A Merry Christ
mas.
And a Happy
New years.

Forget me not
For if you do
I'll kick you
With my darn
old Shoe.

When you get old and
    ugly,
As some people often do.
Remember that you.
have a friend that
    is old and ugly to.

            S.

When the golden sun
    is setting,.
and your heart from
    care is free,
When of thousands
    things you're thinking
well you some times
    think of me.
            S.

PRACTICAL

ENGLISH GRAMMAR

WITH

EXERCISES IN COMPOSITION

BY

MARY F. HYDE

AUTHOR OF A SERIES OF LESSONS IN ENGLISH

BOSTON, U.S.A.

D. C. HEATH & CO., PUBLISHERS

1901

TYPOGRAPHY BY J. S. CUSHING & CO., NORWOOD, MASS.

PRESSWORK BY H. M. PLIMPTON & CO., NORWOOD, MASS.

PREFACE

This book is designed for the higher grades in grammar schools, and for those classes in high schools, academies, and ungraded schools that require a brief, practical, progressive course in English grammar.

The aim of the work is to give the pupil a mastery of the fundamental facts of English grammar, and to lead him to use that knowledge in the interpretation of literature and in the expression of his own thought.

The instruction has been made concrete by the use of illustrative examples. These examples have been selected with great care from the works of the best writers, and they not only serve to make clear the grammatical points under consideration, but also aid in the formation of the pupil's literary taste, and help him to see that the laws of language are derived from the usage of the best writers and speakers.

Abundant and varied exercises for the application of the principles presented are given throughout the book. The pupil is required to show his understanding of the subject by his ability to give original illustrations of the facts studied, as well as to point out and explain the various forms and constructions found in sentences selected from literature.

The selection and arrangement of topics is adapted to give the pupil a clear and comprehensive view of the subject. Part First treats of the Sentence and the Parts of Speech, and lays the foundation for the pupil's mastery of the sentence by emphasizing the fact that it is not the form, but the function, of a word in a sentence that determines the class to which it belongs.

Part Second takes up the subdivisions of the Parts of Speech and Inflection. The chief emphasis is placed upon the main facts, but the attention of the pupil is also directed to such special forms and uses of words as he will be most likely to meet in his reading. Special training is given upon words and forms commonly misused.

Part Third treats of Syntax. It gives the leading constructions of words in the English sentence, with numerous illustrations from literature.

Part Fourth treats of the Structure and Analysis of sentences. It provides for a careful study of clauses in connection with the complex sentence, and contains clear and concise models for oral and written analysis and a great abundance of carefully selected matter for illustration and practice.

Part Fifth relates to Composition. It gives training upon the paragraph, exercises in narration and description, and a special study of letter-writing and related subjects.

My cordial thanks are returned to all who, by criticism or suggestion, have aided in the preparation of this book.

M. F. H.

CONTENTS

PART FIRST

THE SENTENCE AND THE PARTS OF SPEECH

PART SECOND

SUBDIVISIONS OF THE PARTS OF SPEECH AND INFLECTION

CONTENTS

CONTENTS

PART THIRD

Syntax

PART FOURTH

STRUCTURE AND ANALYSIS OF SENTENCES

PART FIFTH

COMPOSITION

APPENDIX

PART FIRST

THE SENTENCE AND THE PARTS OF SPEECH

———o·o·o·o·o———

CHAPTER I

THE SENTENCE

A *sentence* is the expression of a complete thought in words; as, —

1. The fire burns brightly.
2. The sky is clear.

A sentence may —

(1) State or declare something; as, *The leaves are falling.*

(2) Express a command or an entreaty; as, *Look at the leaves.*

(3) Ask a question; as, *What makes the leaves fall?*

(4) Express sudden or strong feeling; as, *How silently the leaves fall!*

A sentence that states or declares something is a *declarative sentence.*

A sentence that expresses a command or an entreaty is an *imperative sentence.*

A sentence that asks a question is an *interrogative sentence.* A sentence that expresses sudden or strong feeling is an *exclamatory sentence.*

EXERCISE 1

In each of the following examples, tell for what the sentence is used and what kind of sentence it is: —

1. Nearly all the night-birds fly on wings that make no noise.
2. Every day is the best day of the year.
3. How the early settlers prized the apple !
4. A friendly eye could never see such faults.
5. Many flowers close their petals during rain.
6. The house was built of stone.
7. We heard the distant roar of the surf.
8. How beautiful is the rain !
9. Night is the time for rest.
10. How many persons entered the room?
11. We could hear the chattering cry of the king-fisher.
12. What an admirable piece of work this is !
13. On the cross beam under the Old South bell
    The nest of a pigeon is builded well.
14. A tear stood in his bright blue eye.
15. I had three fine rosy-cheeked schoolboys for my fellow-passengers.
16. Beware of entrance to a quarrel.
17. Let us do right to all men.
18. Remember the Sabbath day to keep it holy.
19. Few know the use of life before 'tis past.
20. The troops were concealed by a thick wood.
21. The fisheries are the chief support of Yarmouth.

EXERCISE 2

Select from your Readers (1) *three declarative sentences;* (2) *three imperative sentences;* (3) *three interrogative sentences;* (4) *three exclamatory sentences.*

CHAPTER II

SUBJECT AND PREDICATE

In each of the following sentences, tell (1) what the assertion is about; (2) what is said or asserted about the thing named:—

1. Birds fly.
2. Fishes swim.
3. Rain falls.
4. Water evaporates.

Every sentence consists of two parts.[1] One part names that about which something is said, and is called the **subject**; the other part tells what is said or asserted about the thing named by the subject, and is called the **predicate**.

The *subject* of a sentence names that about which something is asserted.

The *predicate* of a sentence tells what is asserted about the person or thing named by the subject.

EXERCISE 3

State the subject and the predicate in each of the following sentences, giving in each case a reason for your statement:—

1. Plants grow.
2. Animals move.
3. Leaves fall.
4. Rivers flow.
5. Parrots talk.
6. Quails whistle.

[1] See Appendix IV, page 322.

CHAPTER III

MODIFIED SUBJECT AND PREDICATE

The subject and the predicate may each be expressed by a single word, or by two or more words; as, —

    1. Birds fly.
    2. Some birds fly swiftly.

In the second sentence above, the word *some* limits the meaning of the word *birds*, by showing that not all birds are meant. The word *swiftly* adds to the meaning of the word *fly*, by showing the manner of flight.

When a word limits the application or adds to the meaning of another word in this manner, it is said to **modify** that word, and is called a **modifier**; as, *this* moment, *kind* words, speak *softly*, step *quickly*.

The subject without modifiers is the *grammatical* or *simple subject;* as, *Leaves* fall.

The grammatical subject with its modifiers is the *logical* or *complete subject;* as, *The dead leaves* fall.

The predicate without modifiers is the *grammatical* or *simple predicate;* as, Time *flies.*

The grammatical predicate with its modifiers is the *logical* or *complete predicate;* as, Time *flies swiftly.*

EXERCISE 4

Name the complete subject and the complete predicate, in each of the following sentences: —

    1. Language is the highest mode of expression.
    2. The first spring wild-flowers yield no honey.

3. The old oaken bucket hangs in the well.

4. The palm tree is found in every country from the Tigris to the Atlantic.

5. The blue smoke widened slowly upward through the quiet August atmosphere.

6. This wonderful tree stood in the centre of an ancient wood.

7. The other colonies were not slow in acting.

8. Two important steps had now to be taken at once.

9. A merciful man considers his beast.

10. The good old year is with the past.

11. All plants of the same kind need the same sort of food.

12. The summer breezes go lightly by.

13. Every individual has a place to fill in the world.

14. A wise son heareth his father's instruction.

CHAPTER IV

ORDER OF SUBJECT AND PREDICATE

I. IN DECLARATIVE SENTENCES

The subject of a declarative sentence is usually placed before the predicate. This order of parts is called the **usual order;** as, —

> *The well-curb* had a Chinese roof.

But sometimes, especially in poetry, this order is **transposed** or **inverted,** and the subject is placed after the predicate; as, —

> Up springs *the lark.*
> Sweet is *the breath of morn.*

EXERCISE 5

Change the following sentences from the transposed order to the usual order, and name the complete subject and the complete predicate in each : —

1. Blessed are the pure in heart.
2. Now fades the glimmering landscape on the sight.
3. On their right was a steep hill.
4.   Into the valley of death
          Rode the six hundred.
5. At the head of the bay is the town.
6. Here will we build our habitations.
7. Behind him came a throng of officers.
8. Up flew the windows all.

II. IN IMPERATIVE SENTENCES

The subject of an imperative sentence is *thou, ye,* or *you.* It is seldom expressed; thus, —

Come into the garden (= [You] come into the garden).

When the subject is expressed, it is usually placed after the verb; as, —

Praise *ye* the Lord.

In familiar language, the subject sometimes comes before the verb; as, —

    You stand here.   *You keep* still.

EXERCISE 6

Copy the following sentences, supplying the subjects that are understood and enclosing them in brackets : —

1. Listen to this account of the fire.
2. Fling wide the gates.

3. Throw part of the cargo overboard.
4. Speak gently to the erring.
5. Cleanse thou me from secret faults.
6. Be not weary in well doing.
7. Rejoice in the prosperity of others.
8. Follow the directions carefully.

III. IN INTERROGATIVE SENTENCES

The subject of an interrogative sentence is usually placed after the predicate, or after the first word of the predicate; as, —

Has *the sun* spots?   Does *the sun* shine?

When an interrogative word is used as the subject, or as a modifier of the subject, the subject and predicate are in the direct order; as, —

Who comes here ?   *Which side* won?

EXERCISE 7

Name the subject and the predicate in each of the following sentences : —

1. Why does the earth become cooler after sunset?
2. Why is it sometimes foggy in the morning?
3. What causes the fog to disappear?
4. What wind is accompanied by a clear sky?
5. Did you ever see a cloudless sky?

IV. IN EXCLAMATORY SENTENCES

Most exclamatory sentences begin with *how* or *what*, and the subject and predicate are often transposed; as, —

> How beautiful is night !
> What an excellent likeness this is !

Sometimes, however, a declarative, imperative, or interrogative sentence is written or printed with the exclamation point at its close, to give greater emphasis to the thought. It is then called an exclamatory sentence; as, —

> The war is actually begun !
> Give me liberty or give me death !
> Who can foretell the result !

EXERCISE 8

In the following examples, (1) tell the kind of each sentence ; (2) name its subject and its predicate. Give a reason for your statements : —

1. How excellent is thy loving-kindness !
2. What a deep-rooted plant it was !
3. How wonderful is sleep !
4. What a crisis had now arrived !
5. Here we are at last !
6. How lightly past hardship sits upon us !
7. What real service to others did you render yesterday?
8. Consider the lilies of the field.
9. Out of the abundance of the heart the mouth speaketh.
10. How blessings brighten as they take their flight !
11. Kind hearts are more than coronets.
12. Truth seeks open dealing.
13. A merry heart maketh a cheerful countenance.
14. Make yourself necessary to somebody.

CHAPTER V

NOUNS

Which words in the following sentences are used as names?

1. Benjamin Franklin discovered electricity.
2. A certain man planted a vineyard.
3. The shadows dance upon the wall.

A word used as a name is a **noun**. A noun may be the name of —

(1) A person; as, *Homer* was a great poet.

(2) A place; as, *Cairo* is the capital of *Egypt*.

(3) A thing we can see, feel, hear, smell, or touch; as, (a) The *stars* are bright. (b) *Ice* is cold. (c) The *bluebird* sings. (d) *Violets* are sweet.

(4) Something that we can think of but cannot perceive by the senses; as, (a) *Kindness* wins friends. (b) *Wisdom* is better than *strength*.

(5) An action; as, *Rowing* expands the chest.

A *noun* is a word used as a name.

EXERCISE 9

In each of the following examples, (1) tell whether the sentence is declarative, imperative, interrogative, or exclamatory; (2) point out the nouns in it, and tell what each names: —

1. He goes on Sunday to the church
   And sits among his boys.

2. How quietly the child sleeps!

3. A large island covered with palms divides the Nile into two branches.

4. His door was always open to the wayfarer.

5. Hear me with patience.

6. From what port did you sail ?

7. He came early in the spring to the settlement of New Plymouth.

8. The breeze comes whispering in our ear,
That dandelions are blossoming near,
That maize has sprouted, that streams are flowing,
That the river is bluer than the sky,
That the robin is plastering his house hard by ;
And if the breeze kept the good news back,
For other couriers we should not lack.

EXERCISE 10

Write (1) *two sentences, each containing the name of a person;* (2) *two sentences, each containing the name of a place ;* (3) *two sentences, each containing the name of a thing perceived by the senses ;* (4) *two sentences, each containing the name of a quality ;* (5) *two sentences, each containing the name of a feeling. Underline the nouns in the sentences written.*

CHAPTER VI

PRONOUNS

For what are the italicized words used in the following sentences ?

1. *I* met a little cottage girl,
She was eight years old, *she* said.

2. "Sisters and brothers, little maid,
   How many may *you* be ?"

3. "How many ? Seven in all," *she* said,
   And wondering looked at *me*.

A word used for a noun is a **pronoun**. By the use of the pronoun, we can avoid the repetition of a noun, and designate a person or thing without naming it. A pronoun may designate —

(1) The speaker or the speaker and others; as, *I, my, me, we, our, us.*

(2) The person or persons addressed; as, *thou, thy, thee, ye, your, you.*

(3) A person or thing, or two or more persons or things, that have been previously mentioned; as, *he, his, him, she, her, hers, it, its, they, their, them.*

A *pronoun* is a word used for a noun.

EXERCISE 11

Point out the pronouns in the following sentences, and state for what each is used: —

1. Train up a child in the way he should go.

2. Nearly all the night insects are comparatively noiseless in their flight.

3. The books remain where you left them.

4. When I turned again to look for the bird, I could not see it.

5. Crinkle-root is spicy, but you must partake of it delicately, or it will bite your tongue.

6. Trust men and they will be true to you; treat them greatly and they will show themselves great.

7. She folded her arms beneath her cloak.

8. As the route of the friends lay in the same direction, they agreed to make the rest of their journey together.

9.   Not a soldier discharged his farewell shot
        O'er the grave where our hero we buried.

10. A belted kingfisher suddenly appeared in the air just in front of me, where he hovered for a moment as if doubtful whether to fly over us and go up the river or to turn about and retreat before us.

EXERCISE 12

Write (1) *two sentences, each containing a pronoun used to designate the speaker;* (2) *two sentences, each containing a pronoun used to designate a person addressed;* (3) *three sentences, each containing a pronoun used for the name of a person or thing spoken of.*

CHAPTER VII

ADJECTIVES

Find in the following sentences words used with nouns to describe or to point out the things named: —

1. A tall shrub grows by the brook.
2. The plant has yellow blossoms.
3. These flowers appear in autumn.

In the examples above, the word *tall* describes the shrub named, in regard to height; the word *yellow* tells the color of the blossoms; *the* limits the application of the noun *plant* to a particular plant; *these* points out the flowers referred to.

A word used to modify the meaning of a noun or pronoun is an **adjective**. An adjective may show —

(1) What kind of thing is named; as, *large* city, *bold* warrior, *merry* heart.

(2) How many things are mentioned; as, *ten* commandments, *twelve* months, *some* lakes, *many* books.

(3) How much of a quantity is referred to; as, *little* rain, *less* time.

(4) What thing is spoken of; as, *this* house, *those* trees, *yonder* cottage.

An *adjective* is a word used to modify the meaning of a noun or pronoun.

EXERCISE 13

Name the adjectives in the following sentences, state the use of each adjective, and tell what it modifies : —

1. Two ships were anchored in the bay.
2. Blue were her eyes as the fairy flax.
3. A wise son maketh a glad father.
4. Brave hearts were ready for bold deeds.
5. These people are honest, kind-hearted, and industrious.
6. The statue is nearly seven feet in height.
7. The wax candles were now lighted, and showed a handsome room, well provided with rich furniture.
8. The doe was a beauty, with slender limbs, not too heavy flanks, round body, and aristocratic head, with small ears, and luminous, intelligent, affectionate eyes.

9.   His withered cheek and tresses gray,
      Seemed to have known a better day.

CHAPTER VIII

VERBS

In the following sentences point out the words that tell or assert something of the thing named : —

1. Birds sing.
2. The wind blows.
3. He is a soldier.

A word that asserts is a **verb**. A verb may assert —

(1) Action; as, Children *play*.

(2) Being or existence; as, God *is*.

(3) State or condition; as, (*a*) The picture *hangs* on the wall. (*b*) The infant *sleeps*.

A *verb* is a word that asserts.

Some verbs consist of more than one word; as, —

A ball *will roll*.   The book *has been found*.

Such compound forms are sometimes called **verb-phrases.**[1]

The word that denotes the person or thing about which the assertion is made is called the **subject** of the verb; as, —

The *gardener* pruned the trees.

EXERCISE 14

Point out the verbs in the following sentences, state what each tells, and name its subject : —

1. The song-birds nearly all build low.
2. The weasel is an enemy of the birds.

[1] See page 27.

3. The curfew tolls the knell of parting day.

4. He springs from his hammock, he flies to the deck.

5. The pigeons fly in great clouds from village to village.

6. The kettle sings, the cat in chorus purrs.

7. They robbed the wild bees of their honey, and chased the deer over the hills.

8. The horses neighed, and the oxen lowed.

9. She pointed to the web of beautifully woven cloth in the loom.

10. A fire blazed brightly on the hearth.

11. The shadows dance upon the wall.

12. The troops marched steadily on.

13.   When breezes are soft and skies are fair,
      I steal an hour from study and care.

14. Thus the night passed. The moon went down; the stars grew pale; the cold day broke; the sun rose.

EXERCISE 15

Write sentences containing the following words used (1) *as nouns;* (2) *as verbs:* —

bark	walk	fear	sail	salt
rock	look	dream	water	hope

EXERCISE 16

Write sentences containing the following words used as the subjects of verbs. Underline the verbs: —

moon	iron	soldier	singer	wind
courage	grocer	river	organ	bell

CHAPTER IX

ADVERBS

In the following sentences point out the words that show *how*, *when*, or *where* actions were performed: —

1. The boat moves slowly.
2. He always spoke the truth.
3. The child stood here.

Give the verb in each sentence, and tell what word modifies its meaning.

A word that modifies the meaning of a verb is an **adverb**.

Sometimes an adverb is used to modify the meaning of an adjective; as, —

It is *very* cold.
The sleeve is *too* short.

Sometimes an adverb is used to modify the meaning of another adverb; as, —

The boat moves *very* slowly.
Do not walk *so* fast.

An *adverb* is a word that modifies the meaning of a verb, an adjective, or another adverb.

EXERCISE 17

Mention the adverbs in the following sentences, and tell what each modifies: —

1. The bell rang sharply.
2. She turned, and looked back.

3. How hard a lesson it is to wait!
4. How silently the snow falls!
5. The common wild birds of the woods were everywhere.
6. Faster and faster we sped.
7. The shower soon passed.
8. The statement is perfectly correct.
9. But we steadfastly gazed on the face of the dead,
   And we bitterly thought of the morrow.
10. Catbirds differ greatly in vocal talent.

EXERCISE 18

Write (1) *five sentences, each containing an adverb modifying a verb;* (2) *three sentences, each containing an adverb modifying an adjective;* (3) *two sentences, each containing an adverb modifying an adverb.*

CHAPTER X

PREPOSITIONS

In the following sentences point out the words that join nouns or pronouns to other words:—

1. They sailed up the river.
2. No one spoke to him.
3. The clock in the steeple struck three.
4. She is fond of music.

A word used with a noun or pronoun to show its relation to some other word in the sentence is called a **preposition**; as, —

The leaves fell *to* the ground.

The noun or pronoun used with a preposition in this manner is called its **object**. A preposition is usually placed before its object, but sometimes it follows it; as, —

The boat is *on* the *shore.* *What* are you looking *at?*

A preposition usually joins a noun or pronoun to —

(1) A verb; as, He *lived by* the *river.*
(2) An adjective; as, They are *ready for battle.*
(3) A noun; as, It is a *package of letters.*

A *preposition* is a word used with a noun or pronoun to show its relation to some other word in the sentence.

EXERCISE 19

Mention the prepositions in the following sentences, tell between what words each shows a relation, and name its object: —

1. A fair little girl sat under a tree.
2. The dining table stood in the centre of the room.
3. The boy was pleased at the prospect of taking a long journey.
4. At midnight I was aroused by the tramp of horses' hoofs in the yard.
5. The habits of our American cuckoo are extremely interesting.
6. Into the street the Piper stept.
7. They were eager for the contest.
8. Every day the starving poor
   Crowded around Bishop Hatto's door.
9. Like the leaves of the forest, when summer is green,
   That host with their banners at sunset were seen.
10. I see the lights of the village
    Gleam through the rain and the mist.

EXERCISE 20

Tell whether the italicized words in the following sentences are adverbs or prepositions, giving reasons in each case : —

1. Is your employer *within?*
2. The work will be done *within* a week.
3. It rolled *down* the hill.
4. Slowly and sadly we laid him *down.*
5. A voice replied far *up* the height.
6. Lift *up* thine eyes unto the hills.
7. They passed *by.*
8. He sat *by* the well.
9. Your hat is *behind* the door.
10. Do not lag *behind.*
11. A beautiful picture hung *above* the altar.
12. The eagle soars *above.*
13. The multitude went before.
14. The cat lay before the fire.

15. *By* thirty hills I hurry *down,*
    Or slip between the ridges,
    By twenty thorps, a little town,
    And half a hundred bridges.

EXERCISE 21

(1) *Write five sentences, each containing a preposition expressing a relation between a verb and a noun.*

(2) *Write five sentences, each containing a preposition expressing a relation between two nouns.*

(3) *Write three sentences, each containing a preposition expressing a relation between an adjective and a noun.*

CHAPTER XI

CONJUNCTIONS

In the following examples, find (1) short sentences joined by the italicized words; (2) similar words or groups of words that are so joined: —

1. The walls are high, *and* the shores are steep.
2. They came, *but* they did not stay.
3. Slowly *and* sadly we laid him down.
4. We have been friends together,
    In sunshine *and* in shade.

A word that connects sentences or similar parts of the same sentence is a **conjunction**. A conjunction may connect —

(1) Two sentences; as, *Be just*, and *fear not*.

(2) Two phrases[1]; as, Through days *of sorrow* and *of mirth*.

(3) Two words; as, (*a*) *Time* and *tide* wait for no man (nouns). (*b*) Her voice was *low* and *sweet* (adjectives). *Sink* or *swim* (verbs). (*c*) Look *before* and *behind* (adverbs).

A *conjunction* is a word that connects sentences, or similar parts of the same sentence.

EXERCISE 22

Point out the conjunctions in the following sentences, and tell what they connect: —

1. The floods came, and the winds blew.
2. Freely we serve, because we freely love.

[1] See page 27.

3. He reached the well, but nobody was there.

4. The ploughman homeward plods his weary way,
   And leaves the world to darkness and to me.

5. She must weep, or she will die.
6. The flames danced and capered in the polished grate.

7. Sink or swim, live or die, survive or perish, I give my heart and my hand to this vote.

8. Three years she grew in sun and shower.

9. The waves beside them danced; but they
   Outdid the sparkling waves in glee.

10. Blessed are the merciful, for they shall obtain mercy.

EXERCISE 23

Show which of the italicized words in the following sentences are prepositions, and which are conjunctions : —

1. They came, *but* they did not remain.
2. He cares for nothing *but* money.
3. All the family were present, *except* one son.
4. *Except* ye repent, ye shall all likewise perish.
5. I have not heard from them *since* yesterday.
6. *Since* you are here, you might remain.
7. The children ran *after* the procession.
8. He came *after* the exercises had closed.
9. The building will be completed *before* the leaves fall.
10. It stands *before* the fireplace.
11. Stay here *until* I come.
12. They will remain abroad *until* November.
13. He died *for* his country.
14. Our bugles sang truce; *for* the night-cloud had lowered.

EXERCISE 24

Write sentences containing conjunctions joining (1) *two sentences;* (2) *two nouns;* (3) *two adjectives;* (4) *two verbs;* (5) *two adverbs.*

CHAPTER XII

INTERJECTIONS

What words in the following sentences form no part of either subject or predicate?

    1. Alas! we have delayed too long.
    2. Hark! was that a knock?
    3. Hurrah! the day is won.

What feeling is expressed by the use of the word *alas?* By the word *hark?* By the word *hurrah?*

A word used to indicate sudden or intense feeling is called an **interjection.** Interjections may express—

(1) Joy; as, *hurrah! huzzah!*
(2) Pain or suffering; as, *ah! oh! alas!*
(3) Surprise; as, *ha! lo! what!*
(4) Disapproval; as, *fie! fudge!*
(5) A desire to call attention; as, *ho! hey! hark!*
                etc., etc.

An *interjection* is a word used to indicate sudden or intense feeling.

EXERCISE 25

Point out the interjections in the following sentences, and tell what they express:—

1. Alas ! I am undone.
2. Away ! we must not linger.
3. Hush ! it is the dead of night.
4. Halloo ! who stands guard here ?
5. Ah ! whence is that flame which now glares on his eye ?
6. Oh ! how many broken bonds of affection were here !
7. But hush ! hark ! a deep sound strikes like a rising knell.
8. Ha ! feel ye not your fingers thrill ?

CHAPTER XIII

REVIEW OF THE PARTS OF SPEECH

Mention some of the different uses of words in a sentence.

What do we call a word that is used as a name ? A word used instead of a noun ? A word that asserts ?

How many classes of words are used as modifiers ? What are these classes called ? How does the adjective differ from the adverb ?

How many kinds of connecting words have been considered ? What are they called ? In what way are prepositions and conjunctions alike ? How do they differ ?

Mention a class of words not grammatically related to the other words in a sentence.

How many kinds of words have been considered ?

Words are divided into classes according to their uses in sentences. These different classes of words are called **parts of speech**. The parts of speech are : —

1. The Noun.   5. The Adverb.
2. The Pronoun.   6. The Preposition.
3. The Adjective.   7. The Conjunction.
4. The Verb.   8. The Interjection.

EXERCISE 26

Distinguish between the uses of the italicized words in each of the following examples, and name the part of speech of each word: —

1. Then rushed the steel to *battle* driven. The troops appeared in *battle* array.

2. *Farewell!* a long *farewell*, to all my greatness. Not a soldier discharged his *farewell* shot.

3. It was over in one *second*. Omit the *second* stanza. I *second* the motion.

4. He is as *good* as he is strong. Who will show us any *good?*

5. They visited a *far* country. *Far* flashed the red artillery.

6. This is the *best* answer that was given.

> He prayeth *best* who loveth *best*
> All things both great and small.

7. The horse is a *fast* walker. The child is *fast* asleep. When ye *fast*, be not, as the hypocrites, of a sad countenance. The shades of night were falling *fast*.

8. He is *still* here. Now came *still* evening on. There is a good fire, *still* the room is cold.

To the Teacher. — Give additional exercises, if they are needed, to impress the fact, that it is not the form of a word, but its use in a sentence, that determines what *part of speech* the word is.

CHAPTER XIV

PHRASES

In the following examples, find combinations of words used like parts of speech: —

1. The leader is a *courageous* man.
2. The leader is a man *of courage*.
3. What did you see *there?*
4. What did you see *in that place?*

A combination of words performing a distinct office in a sentence, but having neither subject nor predicate, is a *phrase.*

A phrase that performs the office of an adjective is an *adjective phrase;* as, The leaves *on the tree* are green.

A phrase that performs the office of an adverb is an *adverbial phrase;* as, The boys are skating *on the pond.*

EXERCISE 27

In the following sentences, point out the adjective phrases and the adverbial phrases: —

1. The cargo of the ship is valuable.
2. There groups of merry children played.
3. I stand upon my native hills again.
4. The road to the river is straight.
5. The command of the general must be obeyed.
6. Two officers of the company were killed in battle.
7. The dress of the fugitive betrayed him.
8. The ships sailed down the bay.

EXERCISE 28

Re-write the following sentences, substituting equivalent phrases for the italicized adjectives : —

1. It was a *valuable* stone.
2. He wore a *fur* coat.
3. *Beautiful* paintings adorned the walls.
4. We attended the *water-color* exhibition.
5. An *iron* bridge spanned the stream.
6. The piano has a *mahogany* case.
7. The captain was a *courageous* man.
8. A *prudent* man foreseeth the evil.

Example. — It was a *valuable* stone.

It was a stone *of great value.*

EXERCISE 29

Re-write the following sentences, substituting equivalent phrases for the italicized adverbs : —

1. The work will be completed *soon.*
2. He opened the door *cautiously.*
3. We shall sit *here* during the address.
4. Do not stand *there.*
5. He copied the exercise *carefully.*
6. Can you give me the address *now* ?
7. They spoke *kindly* to the boy.
8. The dress was made *neatly.*

Example. — The work will be completed *soon.*

The work will be completed *in a short time.*

CHAPTER XV

CLAUSES

Tell how many assertions are made in each of the following sentences, and name the subject and the predicate in each assertion : —

1. When the signal was given, the boats started.
2. The building was condemned, because it was unsafe.
3. I believe that he is honest.

A combination of words performing a distinct office in a sentence, and having a subject and a predicate, is a *clause*.

A clause that expresses the leading or principal thought of a sentence is an *independent* or *principal clause*; as —

They trimmed the lamps as the sun went down.

A clause that depends upon some other part of the sentence for its full meaning is a *dependent* or *subordinate clause*; as —

They trimmed the lamps *as the sun went down.*

EXERCISE 30

In each of the following sentences, point out the principal clause and the subordinate clause: —

1. You may remain where you are.
2. Speak as you think.
3. If our cause is just, we shall succeed.
4. What his decision will be is uncertain.
5. Remember what has been done for you.
6. She listened attentively while he was speaking.
7. When the fire was extinguished, the crowd dispersed.
8. He left the room as I entered the door.

EXERCISE 31

Find the subordinate clauses in the following sentences, and tell whether they are used like adjectives, like adverbs, or like nouns : —

1. They that touch pitch will be defiled.
2. Forgive us our debts as we forgive our debtors.
3. Do the duty which lies nearest to thee.
4. That he was brave cannot be denied.
5. We hope that you will succeed.
6. Make hay while the sun shines.

A clause that performs the office of an adjective is an *adjective clause.*

A clause that performs the office of an adverb is an *adverbial clause.*

A clause that performs the office of a noun is a *noun clause.*

EXERCISE 32

Point out the adjective clauses and the adverbial clauses in the following sentences, and tell what they modify : —

1. He that walketh uprightly walketh surely.
2. The upright man speaks as he thinks.
3. Before the firemen came, the building was destroyed.
4. When you enter the room, close the door softly.
5. Happy is the man that findeth wisdom.
6. The box, which had been locked, was now opened.
7. The tree lies where it fell.
8. The wind bloweth where it listeth.

PART SECOND

SUBDIVISIONS OF THE PARTS OF SPEECH AND INFLECTION

———o◦❀◦o———

CHAPTER XVI

CLASSES OF NOUNS

I. PROPER AND COMMON NOUNS

Point out in the following sentences (1) the nouns that name special persons or things, (2) the nouns that apply to every one of a class of persons or things: —

1. The White House is the official residence of the President of the United States. The corner-stone of the White House was laid by General Washington.
2. Paris is called the finest city in the world.
3. Longfellow is the most popular American poet.

A name that belongs to an individual person or thing is a *proper noun;* as, *Clarence, New York, Thursday, Lake George.*

Proper nouns and words derived from them begin with capital letters. When a proper noun is made up of two or more words, each word generally begins with a capital letter.

A name that applies to every one of a class of persons or things is a *common noun;* as, *boy, city, day, lake.*

(1) *Write sentences containing a name that applies to every one of a class of (a) persons; (b) places; (c) buildings.*

(2) *Write sentences containing the name of an individual (a) poet; (b) statesman; (c) city; (d) country; (e) lake.*

II. COLLECTIVE NOUNS

Point out the nouns in the following sentences that name collections of persons or things, and tell of what each collection is composed: —

1. The speaker was afraid to face the audience.
2. The Assembly adjourned at twelve o'clock.
3. There is no flock, however watched and tended,
   But one dead lamb is there. — LONGFELLOW.
4. Are fleets and armies necessary to a work of love and reconciliation? — PATRICK HENRY.

A noun that in the singular number applies to a collection of persons or things is a *collective noun;* as, *family, jury, swarm.*

Collective nouns are usually common; but when a collective noun is applied to an individual body, as in the second example above, it is proper.

Write sentences containing words used to name a collection of —

ships	soldiers	sailors	wolves	sheep
bees	thieves	buffaloes	fish	chickens

III. ABSTRACT NOUNS

Point out each word in the following examples that is the name of a quality or condition of a person or thing : —

1. The length of a river.
2. The bravery of the soldier.
3. The growth of the plant.

A noun that is the name of a quality, action, or condition of a person or thing, apart from the person or thing itself, is an *abstract noun ;* as, *goodness, happiness.*

An abstract noun that is the name of an action is sometimes called a **verbal noun ;** as, *walking, singing.*

Abstract nouns are formed —

(1) From adjectives ; as, *brightness* from *bright ; honesty* from *honest ; patience* from *patient.*

(2) From verbs ; as, *invention* from *invent ; singing* from *sing.*

(3) From nouns ; as *childhood* from *child ; knavery* from *knave.*

EXERCISE 35

Point out each noun in the following sentences, and state the class to which it belongs : —

1. The child's illness is of an alarming nature.
2. Wisdom is better than strength.
3. He has repented of his folly
4. The time of the singing of birds has come.
5. His writing was illegible.

6. Charity covereth a multitude of sins.

7. How poor are they that have not patience !

8. How little they knew of the depth, and the strength, and the intensity of that feeling of resistance to illegal acts of power, which possessed the whole American people !

EXERCISE 36

Write the following words in columns, and opposite each word place the corresponding abstract noun : —

industrious	weak	bright	warm	honest
temperate	walk	courageous	true	wise
sweet	judge	beautiful	just	innocent
proud	conceal	deceive	high	dull
long	please	learn	hard	pure

CHAPTER XVII

INFLECTION OF NOUNS — NUMBER

Some words are changed in form to denote a change in their meaning or their relation to the rest of the sentence ; as, *book, books ; boy, boy's ; you, your ; write, wrote.*

The change in the form of a word to denote a change of meaning or relation is called *inflection.*

The inflection of a noun or pronoun is called its **declension ;** the inflection of an adjective or adverb is called its **comparison ;** the inflection of a verb is called its **conjugation.**

Tell how many forms each noun in the following examples has, and whether each form denotes one or more than one: —

| book | watch | fox | piano | potato |
| books | watches | foxes | pianos | potatoes |

The distinction between one and more than one is called *number*.

The form which denotes one thing is the *singular number;* as, *bird*, *match*, *leaf*.

The form which denotes more than one thing is the *plural number;* as, *birds*, *matches*, *leaves*.

NUMBER FORMS OF NOUNS

Give the plural of each of the following nouns, and tell how it is formed: —

bird	canto	chimney	cuff
boat	piano	day	gulf
trap	solo	key	roof
paper	folio	alley	life

I. Nouns regularly form the plural by adding *s* to the singular; as, *river*, *rivers; halo*, *halos; valley*, *valleys; chief*, *chiefs*.

II. Nouns ending in a hissing sound like that of *s, x, sh, ch,* and *z,* form the plural by adding *es* to the singular; as, *gas*, *gases; tax*, *taxes; thrush*, *thrushes; match*, *matches; topaz*, *topazes*.

EXERCISE 37

Write the following words in columns, and opposite each word write its plural form: —

battle	tack	marble	bridge	arch
glass	race[1]	rose	brooch	niche
latch	fish	mesh	prize	hoe
box	larch	lens	ditch	hedge
chorus	metal	rush	bush	ice

Which words in the list above add *es*?

III. **Most nouns ending in *o* add *s* to the singular to form the plural; some add *es*; and a few add either *s* or *es*.**

EXERCISE 38

Form the plurals of the following words by adding s to the singular: —

alto	cuckoo	halo	oratorio	soprano
banjo	duodecimo	junto	piano	stiletto
cameo	dynamo	memento	portfolio	trio
canto	embryo	nuncio	quarto	two
chromo	folio	octavo	solo	tyro

The plurals of *bravo*, *lasso*, *mosquito*, and *motto* are formed by adding either *s* or *es;* as *bravos*[2] or *bravoes; lassos* or *lassoes; mosquitos* or *mosquitoes; mottos* or *mottoes.*

EXERCISE 39

Form the plurals of these nouns by adding **es** *to the singular:* —

---

[1] Words ending in silent *e* drop the final *e* when *es* is added.

[2] The form that is preferred is placed first.

| echo | embargo | negro | tomato | torpedo |
| hero | mulatto | potato | tornado | veto |

The plurals of *buffalo*, *cargo*, *domino*, and *volcano* are formed by adding either *es* or *s;* as, *buffaloes* or *buffalos; cargoes* or *cargos; dominoes* or *dominos; volcanoes* or *volcanos*.

EXERCISE 40

Form the plurals of eight nouns that may add either **s** *or* **es**, *placing the preferred form first.*

Give the ending of the singular nouns in the following examples, and tell how their plurals are formed: —

| city | story | day | chimney |
| cities | stories | days | chimneys |

IV. **Nouns ending in *y* preceded by a vowel, add *s* to the singular, to form the plural; nouns ending in *y* preceded by a consonant, change *y* to *ies*;** as *boy, boys; chimney, chimneys; city, cities; lily lilies.*

EXERCISE 41

Write sentences containing the plurals of the following words: —

body	colloquy [1]	berry	jury	alley
copy	soliloquy	ferry	journey	pulley
daisy	vanity	lily	mystery	duty
fly	buoy	quay	donkey	Marcy [2]

[1] *Qu* stands for *kw*, hence the *y* of *colloquy* and *soliloquy* is really not preceded by a vowel sound.

[2] Many proper names do not follow the rule, but simply add *s*; as, *Henrys, Stacys.*

How are the singular nouns in the following examples changed to make each mean more than one?—

proof	gulf	fife
proofs	gulfs	fifes

V. **Most nouns ending in *f* or *fe* form the plural by adding *s* to the singular ;** as, *roof, roofs ; safe, safes.*

The following nouns change *f* or *fe* to *ves :* —

beef	knife	self	thief[2]
calf	leaf	sheaf	wharf[2]
elf	life	shelf	wife
half	loaf	staff[1]	wolf

EXERCISE 42

Make (1) *a list of ten nouns, ending in* **f** *or* **fe**, *that form their plurals by the addition of* **s** *; and* (2) *a list of ten other nouns that form their plurals in* **ves**.

CHAPTER XVIII

IRREGULAR PLURALS OF NOUNS

Tell how the plurals below are formed: —

man	foot	mouse	ox	child
men	feet	mice	oxen	children

VI. **Some nouns form the plural by changing the vowel of the singular ;** as, *man, men ; goose, geese ; tooth, teeth ; foot, feet ; mouse, mice* (also changes *s* to *c*).

---

[1] Staff (a stick or pole), *staves* or *staffs ;* staff (a body of officers), *staffs.*
[2] Wharf, *wharves* or *wharfs.*

In a few nouns the plural ends in *en*[1]; as *ox, oxen ; brother, brethren ; child, children.*

Give the number of each italicized noun in the following examples, and notice its form : —

     1. A *sheep* before her shearers is dumb.
     2. The *sheep* are feeding in the pasture.

VII. Some nouns have the same form in both numbers ; as, *deer, sheep, swine.*

Other nouns which have the same form in both numbers are *brace, dozen, head, pair,* and *yoke* when used after numerals, and *head, sail, cannon, fish, trout,* and *heathen,* when used in a special or a collective sense.

VIII. Some nouns are used only in the plural ; as, —

aborigines	clothes	scissors	tidings	trousers
assets	dregs	thanks	tongs	vitals

IX. Some nouns plural in form are now generally used as singulars ; as, —

amends	economics	measles	physics
ethics	mathematics	news	politics

X. Some nouns ending in *s* or *es* are not plurals ; as, *alms, eaves, riches.*

---

[1] The old plural *kine* (= kyen) is still used in poetry, and such forms as *eyen* (eyes), *hosen* (hose), and *shoon* (shoes) are found in several dialects.

XI. **Some nouns have two plural forms differing in meaning ; as :—**

brother, *brothers* (by blood) ; *brethren* (by association).
cannon, *cannons* (separately) ; *cannon* (collectively).
die, *dies* (stamps for coining) ; *dice* (cubes for gaming).
fish, *fishes* (separately) ; *fish* (collectively).
genius, *geniuses* (men of genius) ; *genii* (spirits).
index, *indexes* (tables of reference) ; *indices* (signs in algebra).
penny, *pennies* (number of coins) ; *pence* (amount in value).

EXERCISE 43

Write sentences containing the plurals of the following nouns, and tell how each plural is formed :—

woman	foot	cannon	shad	deer
tooth	ox	mouse	fish	genius
sheaf	enemy	buoy	crutch	reef
wharf	colloquy	envoy	life	fife

EXERCISE 44

(1) *Tell which of the following nouns are used in the singular, and which in the plural.*

(2) *Write sentences illustrating their correct use :—*

alms	eaves	politics	thanks
amends	dregs	riches	tidings
aborigines	mathematics	scissors	tongs
clothes	news	shears	victuals

EXERCISE 45

Make a list of the following nouns, and write opposite each its singular : —

genii	geniuses	pence	brethren	indices
beeves	brothers	fishes	wharves	pennies
lives	indexes	women	staves	halves
cannons	elves	sheaves	dice	dies

CHAPTER XIX

PLURALS OF COMPOUNDS

Tell how each plural form below is made from the singular : —

spoonful	brother-in-law	man-servant
spoonfuls	brothers-in-law	men-servants

XII. Some compound nouns form the plural like single words, others make the principal word plural, and a few change both words ; as, *cupful, cupfuls ; mother-in-law, mothers-in-law ; woman-servant, women-servants.*

EXERCISE 46

Write the singulars of the following nouns, and tell how their plurals are formed : —

I.

Brahmans [1]	forget-me-nots	merchantmen
cupfuls	Frenchmen	mouse-traps
dormice	Germans	Normans

[1] The words *Brahman, German, Mussulman, Ottoman,* and *talisman* are not compounds of *man.*

Englishmen	grandfathers	stepsons
fellow-servants	handfuls	talismans
fishermen	major-generals	tooth-brushes

II.

aides-de-camp	fathers-in-law	men-of-war
attorneys-at-law	hangers-on	sisters-in-law
commanders-in-chief	knights-errant	sons-in-law

III.

| knights-templars | men-servants | women-servants |

XIII. **When a title is prefixed to a proper name, the compound may be made plural by changing either the title or the name; as, the *Misses* Brown, the *Messrs.* Gray; or the Miss *Browns*, the Mr. *Grays*.**

The title is always made plural when it is used with two or more names; as, *Messrs.* Stone and Wood; *Generals* Grant and Lee.

XIV. **Letters, figures, and signs add the apostrophe (') and s, to form the plural; as, Dot the *i's;* Cancel the *5's;* Write the +*'s* on a straight line.**

EXERCISE 47

Write the plurals of the following compounds. —

countryman	maid-servant	man-trap
horseshoe	mother-in-law	toothpick
four-per-cent	mouthful	attorney-general
goose-quill	footboy	Miss Hill
journeyman	footman	Mr. North

CHAPTER XX

NOUNS WITH FOREIGN PLURALS

XV. **Many nouns taken from foreign languages retain their original plurals;** as: —

SINGULAR	PLURAL	SINGULAR	PLURAL
alumnus	alumni	genus	genera
analysis	analyses	index	indices
animalculum	animalcula	larva	larvæ
antithesis	antitheses	memorandum	memoranda
apex	apices	nebula	nebulæ
axis	axes	parenthesis	parentheses
basis	bases	phenomenon	phenomena
cherub	cherubim	radius	radii
crisis	crises	seraph	seraphim
datum	data	stratum	strata
erratum	errata	terminus	termini
focus	foci	thesis	theses
formula	formulæ	vertebra	vertebræ
fungus	fungi	vertex	vertices
genius	genii	vortex	vortices

Some foreign words which are in common use form the plural in the usual way, often with a difference of meaning; as *formulas, indexes, geniuses.*

EXERCISE 48

(1) *Make a list of the foregoing singular nouns from foreign languages, and opposite each write from memory its plural.*

(2) *Write (a) five nouns that are used only in the plural;*

(*b*) *two nouns plural in form that are used in the singular;*
(*c*) *three nouns having the same form in both numbers.*

CHAPTER XXI

INFLECTION OF NOUNS—GENDER

Which words in the following list denote males? Which
denote females?

man	father	host	man-servant
woman	mother	hostess	maid-servant

The distinction between words to denote sex is called
gender.

A noun that denotes a male is of the *masculine gender;*
as, *man, heir.*

A noun that denotes a female is of the *feminine gender;*
as, *woman, heiress.*

A noun that may denote either a male or a female is generally
said to be of the *common gender*[1]; as, *parent, friend, robin.*

A noun that denotes a thing neither male nor female is of
the *neuter gender;* as, *book, sky, joy.*

The gender of nouns is distinguished in three ways:—

(1) By different words; as,—

MASCULINE	FEMININE	MASCULINE	FEMININE
bachelor	maid	earl	countess
boy	girl	father	mother
brother	sister	gentleman	lady
buck	doe	hart	roe

[1] Some grammarians do not recognize *common gender.*

MASCULINE	FEMININE	MASCULINE	FEMININE
husband	wife	ram	ewe
king	queen	sir	madam
monk	nun	son	daughter
lord	lady	stag	hind
nephew	niece	uncle	aunt
papa	mamma	wizard	witch

(2) **By different endings.** The chief feminine ending is **ess**.

Some nouns form the feminine by simply adding the suffix **ess** to the masculine; as, —

baron	baroness	Jew	Jewess
count	countess	lion	lioness
deacon	deaconess	patron	patroness
heir	heiress	priest	priestess
host	hostess	shepherd	shepherdess

Other nouns shorten the ending of the masculine, or make other changes, before adding **ess**; as, —

actor	actress	abbot	abbess
benefactor	benefactress	duke	duchess
enchanter	enchantress	emperor	empress
hunter	huntress	governor	governess
preceptor	preceptress	marquis	marchioness
tiger	tigress	master	mistress
waiter	waitress	negro	negress

A few other feminine endings, such as **ine, a,** and **trix,** appear in words taken from foreign languages; as, —

MASCULINE	FEMININE	MASCULINE	FEMININE
hero	heroine	infante	infanta
Joseph	Josephine	signor	signora
Paul	Pauline	sultan	sultana
Augustus	Augusta	administrator	administratrix
czar	czarina	executor	executrix
don	donna	testator	testatrix

(3) **By prefixing or annexing words indicating the sex;**
as, —

MASCULINE	FEMININE
man-servant	maid-servant
men-singers	women-singers
he-goat	she-goat
cock-sparrow	hen-sparrow
peacock	peahen

EXERCISE 49

*Make a list of all the masculine nouns mentioned in the
foregoing lists, and opposite each write from memory the
corresponding feminine noun.*

EXERCISE 50

*Point out the masculine, the feminine, and the neuter
nouns in the following sentences, and tell which nouns may
denote either males or females : —*

1. We learned the ways of the fish, the birds, the bees, the
winds, the clouds, the flowers.

2. Night closed in, but still no guest arrived.

3. Leaving the boatmen at the camp, I spent the greater part
of the night in the very heart of a jungle.

4. Temperance and labor are the two best physicians of man.

5. Though Grandfather was old and gray-haired, yet his heart leaped with joy whenever little Alice came fluttering, like a butterfly, into the room. — HAWTHORNE.

6. I have had playmates, I have had companions.

—CHARLES LAMB.

7. Brethren, the sower's task is done. — BRYANT.

8. I rise, my Lords, to declare my sentiments on this most solemn and serious subject. — BURKE.

9. Little Effie shall go with me to-morrow to the green,
   And you'll be there, too, mother, to see me made the Queen.

— TENNYSON.

10.   Brothers, sisters, husbands, wives,
        Followed the Piper for their lives. — ROBERT BROWNING.

11. The lamps shone o'er fair women and brave men. — BYRON.

12.   What would we give to our beloved ?
        The hero's heart, to be unmoved,
            The poet's star-tuned harp, to sweep,
        The patriot's voice, to teach and rouse,
        The monarch's crown, to light the brows ? —
            He giveth His beloved sleep. — E. B. BROWNING.

CHAPTER XXII

INFLECTION OF NOUNS — CASE

Tell the subjects of the verbs in the following sentences : —

1. The boy bought a watch.
2. An officer caught the thief.
3. Birds build nests.

What did the boy buy? *Whom* did the officer catch? *What* do birds build?

The noun or pronoun that denotes the person or thing receiving the action expressed by a verb is called the **object** of the verb.

State the offices of the italicized words in the following: —

> 1. We followed the *shepherd's* dog.
> 2. The *horse's* bridle is broken.

When a word is used to show to whom or to what something belongs, it is said to denote possession.

Find in the following sentences a noun used (1) as the subject of a verb; (2) as the object of a verb; (3) as the object of a preposition; (4) to denote possession: —

> 1. The boy stood by the door.
> 2. He heard his father's voice.
> 3. A wave upset the boat.

The relation which a noun or pronoun bears to some other word in the sentence is called *case*.

A noun or pronoun used as the subject of a verb is in the *nominative case*; as, —

> The *bell* rang.   *I* hear a lark.

A noun or pronoun used to show possession is in the *possessive case*; as, —

> The *child's* eyes are blue.   She is *my* friend.

A noun or pronoun used as the object of a verb or of a preposition is in the *objective case*; as, —

> They launched the *vessel*.   Come with *me*.

How many case forms have the nouns in the foregoing examples? Which one is indicated by inflection? The possessive case of nouns is the only one that has a special form.

Nouns are inflected for number and for the possessive case.

A noun is said to be **declined** when its number and case forms are regularly arranged; as,—

DECLENSION OF A NOUN

	SINGULAR	PLURAL
Nom.	boy	boys
Poss.	boy's	boys'
Obj.	boy	boys

EXERCISE 51

State the kind, the gender, the number, and the case of the nouns in the following sentences: —

1. This tree stood in the centre of an ancient wood.
2. The waves rush in on every side.
3. Grandfather's chair stood by the fireside.
4. The stranger shook his head mournfully.
5. Birds have wonderfully keen eyes.
6. He shook his head, shouldered the rusty firelock, and with a heart full of trouble and anxiety turned his steps homeward.
7. Dark lightning flashed from Roderick's eye. — SCOTT.
8. When the rock was hid by the surge's swell,
   The mariners heard the warning bell. — SOUTHEY.
9. The rude forefathers of the hamlet sleep. — GRAY.
10. They shook the depths of the desert gloom. — HEMANS.

EXERCISE 52

(1) *Write five sentences, each containing a noun in the nominative case.*

(2) *Write five sentences, each containing a noun in the possessive case.*

(3) *Write five sentences, each containing a noun in the objective case.*

CHAPTER XXIII

POSSESSIVE CASE

Point out the nouns that are in the possessive case, and tell how each possessive is formed : —

1. She knelt by the lady's side.
2. The ladies' gallery is closed.
3. Men's voices were heard.

(1) **Add the apostrophe and *s* ('*s*) to a singular noun, to form the possessive ;** as, *boy, boy's ; man, man's.*

The *s* is sometimes omitted in poetry for the sake of the metre ; and it is also omitted in a few words where too many hissing sounds would come together ; as, for *conscience'* sake ; for *righteousness'* sake ; for *Jesus'* sake.

(2) **Add the apostrophe (') to a plural noun ending in *s*, to form the possessive ;** as, *boys, boys' ; ladies, ladies'.*

(3) **Add the apostrophe and *s* ('*s*) to a plural noun not ending in *s*, to form the possessive ;** as, *men, men's ; children, children's.*

The possessive sign does not always denote possession. It is used to show authorship, origin, kind, etc.; as, *Lowell's* poems; the *sun's* rays; *men's* clothing.

EXERCISE 53

Point out the nouns in these sentences, tell how each is used, and name its case: —

1. The lark's song rang in her ears.
2. The sound of horses' hoofs was heard in the distance.
3. The scene brought to mind an old writer's account of Christmas preparations.
4. The incidents of the Revolution plentifully supplied the barber's customers with topics of conversation.
5. The boy rang the janitor's bell.
6. A burst of laughter came from the servants' hall.
7. I noted but two warblers' nests during the season.

8.   Vainly the fowler's eye
Might mark thy distant flight to do thee wrong. — BRYANT.

9. He felt that his little daughter's love was worth a thousand times more than he had gained by the Golden Touch. — HAWTHORNE.

EXERCISE 54

Write in parallel columns the possessive singular, and the possessive plural forms of the following words: —

sister	woman	boy	girl
mother	wife	soldier	son
bee	bird	friend	teacher
poet	child	man	judge

CHAPTER XXIV

POSSESSIVE CASE OF COMPOUNDS

Tell how the possessive case is formed in the following compound words and phrases: —

1. The lieutenant-governor's revery had now come to an end.
2. Bright and Dun's window is filled with flowers.
3. They are reading Green's and Macaulay's histories.

(4) Compound nouns, words in apposition,[1] and phrases regarded as compound, add the possessive sign to the last word only; as, my *brother-in-law's* house; for thy *servant David's* sake; *somebody else's* hat.

(5) Two or more connected nouns implying joint possession add the possessive sign to the last noun only; as, *William and Mary's* reign; *Mason and Dixon's* line.

(6) Each of two or more connected nouns implying separate possession must take the possessive sign; as, *Webster's and Worcester's* dictionaries; *Longfellow's and Lowell's* poems.

EXERCISE 55

Explain the possessives in the following examples: —

1. In my Father's house are many mansions.
2. Hope vanished from Fitz-James's eye. — Scott.
3.   Enough, enough; sit down and share
         A soldier's couch, a soldier's fare. — Scott.
4. A man's first care should be to avoid the reproaches of his own heart. — Addison.

[1] See page 183.

5. This happened after General Washington's departure from Cambridge.

6. Many a young man ransacked the garret, and brought forth his great-grandfather's sword, corroded with rust and stained with the blood of King Philip's War. — HAWTHORNE.

7. The rest of the house was in the French taste of Charles the Second's time. — IRVING.

8. The grocers', butchers', and fruiterers' shops were thronged with customers. — IRVING.

9. Hither they came, from the cornfields, from the clearing in the forest, from the blacksmith's forge, from the carpenter's workshop, and from the shoemaker's seat. — HAWTHORNE.

10. Let all the ends thou aim'st at be thy country's,
    Thy God's, and truth's. — SHAKESPEARE.

11. What good woman does not laugh at her husband's or father's jokes and stories time after time? — THACKERAY.

12. These are Clan-Alpine's warriors true. — SCOTT.

13. I dined with a party of gentlemen at my friend Mr. James Russell Lowell's. — HOLMES.

14. If to do were as easy as to know what were well to do, chapels had been churches, and poor men's cottages princes' palaces. — SHAKESPEARE.

15. The groves were God's first temples. — BRYANT.

EXERCISE 56

(1.) *Write five sentences, each containing connected nouns denoting joint possession.*

(2.) *Write five sentences, each containing connected nouns denoting separate possession.*

CHAPTER XXV

SUBSTITUTE FOR THE POSSESSIVE INFLECTION

Possession is sometimes indicated by the objective case with the preposition **of**; as, The voice *of the speaker*, for the *speaker's* voice.

This form is generally used in speaking of things without life; as, The lid *of the box;* the bank *of the river.*

This form is preferred also in speaking of persons, when the possessive form would be ambiguous or awkward; as, The wife *of one of my brothers.*

When a thing is personified,[1] the possessive sign is generally used, particularly by the poets; as, —

> Go forth, under the open sky, and list
> To *Nature's* teachings.— BRYANT.

Certain words and phrases denoting a period of time take the possessive case also; as, A *day's* journey; a *week's* vacation; six *months'* interest.

Of is sometimes used before the possessive form of a noun or pronoun, making a sort of double possessive; as, A cousin *of Richard's;* a friend *of mine.*

EXERCISE 57

*Explain fully the case of each noun in the following sentences, and point out the examples in which possession is indicated by the objective case with the preposition **of**: —*

---

[1] When an inanimate thing has ascribed to it the attributes of a person, it is said to be **personified**.

1. I flew to the pleasant fields traversed so oft
    In life's morning march, when my bosom was young.
                                            — CAMPBELL.

2. He has not learned the lesson of life who does not every day surmount a fear. — EMERSON.

3. The trade of America had increased far beyond the speculations of the most sanguine imaginations. — BURKE.

4. The poetry of earth is never dead. — KEATS.

5. Either measure would have cost no more than a day's debate. — BURKE.

6. They came without a moment's delay.

7. She has had two years' experience.

8. He likes neither winter's snow nor summer's heat.

EXERCISE 58

Select from your Reader —

(1) Five sentences in which possession is indicated by the objective case with the preposition **of**.

(2) Five other sentences in which possession is indicated by the use of the possessive sign.

CHAPTER XXVI

HOW TO PARSE NOUNS

To **parse** a word is to describe it by stating (1) the part of speech it is; (2) its inflection, if it has any;[1] and (3) its syntax, or grammatical relations to other words in the sentence.

---

[1] Since nouns have no forms to distinguish person, the **person** of nouns is discussed in connection with the personal pronoun. See page 58.

To parse a noun, state —

(1) Its **class**. (3) Its **gender**.
(2) Its **number**. (4) Its **case**.
(5) Its **syntax** or **construction** — use in the sentence.

EXAMPLE. — His *eyes* sparkled with *joy* when he heard *Jason's reply*.

1. *Eyes* is a noun, common, plural number, neuter gender, and nominative case — subject of the verb *sparkled*.[1]

2. *Joy* is a noun, abstract, singular number, neuter gender, and objective case — object of the preposition *with*.

3. *Jason's* is a noun, proper, singular number, masculine gender, and possessive case — depending upon the noun *reply*.

4. *Reply* is a noun, common, singular number, neuter gender, and objective case — object of the verb *heard*.

EXERCISE 59

Parse the nouns in the following sentences : —

1. The lights of the church shone through the door.
2. Nell and her grandfather rose from the ground, and took the track through the wood. — DICKENS.
3. The rude forefathers of the hamlet sleep. — GRAY.
4. I bring fresh showers for the thirsting flowers. — SHELLEY.
5. Strong reasons make strong actions. — SHAKESPEARE.
6. I stood in Venice, on the Bridge of Sighs. — BYRON.

[1] When the pupil is familiar with the different steps, a briefer method of parsing may be followed ; thus, *Eyes* is a noun, common, plural, neuter, nominative, subject of the verb *sparkled*.

7. I now bade a reluctant farewell to the old hall.—IRVING.

8. A great deal of talent is lost in the world for the want of a little courage.—SYDNEY SMITH.

9. The eyes of the sleepers waxed deadly and chill.—BYRON.

10. Is Saul also among the prophets?—BIBLE.

11. The doe lifted her head a little with a quick motion, and turned her ear to the south.—C. D. WARNER.

12. They had now reached the road which turns off to Sleepy Hollow; but Gunpowder, who seemed possessed with a demon, instead of keeping up it, made an opposite turn, and plunged headlong down hill to the left.—IRVING.

13. 'Tis the middle of night by the castle clock,
    And the owls have awakened the crowing cock.
                                        —COLERIDGE.

14. A soft answer turneth away wrath.—BIBLE.

15. Some have even learned to do without happiness, and instead thereof have found blessedness.—CARLYLE.

16. The lowing herd winds slowly o'er the lea.—GRAY.

17. Reading maketh a full man, conversation a ready man, and writing an exact man.—BACON.

18. Charity beareth all things, believeth all things, hopeth all things, endureth all things.—BIBLE.

CHAPTER XXVII

REVIEW OF NOUNS

EXERCISE 60

What is a noun? Mention the two leading classes of nouns and tell the difference between these classes. What is a collective noun? What is an abstract noun? State three ways in which abstract nouns are formed, and illustrate by examples.

What is meant by inflection? To what do the inflections of nouns relate?

How do most nouns form the plural? Mention other ways in which nouns form their plurals, and illustrate by example.

Give the plural of *watch, piano, potato, donkey, lily, loaf, roof, tooth, ox, sheep.*

Distinguish between the meaning of *brothers* and *brethren; fishes* and *fish; indexes* and *indices; pennies* and *pence.*

State three ways in which compound nouns form the plural, and illustrate by examples.

Give the plural of *larva, alumnus, axis, beau, bandit, seraph.* Why do these nouns not form their plurals in the usual way?

What is gender? How many genders are there, and what does each denote? Mention three ways in which the gender of nouns is distinguished.

Give the feminine nouns corresponding to the nouns *hart, monk, nephew, host, master, governor, executor, hero, man-servant.*

Tell the gender of each of the following nouns, if it has any: *woman, heiress, landlord, doe, waitress, czar, administratrix, guest, friend, witness, cousin, sun, wind, table, house.*

How many cases have nouns? What determines the case of a noun? Which case has a special form? How is the possessive case of nouns formed? How is the possessive formed in compound words and phrases? How may possession be indicated without the possessive form? When is this way preferable?

CHAPTER XXVIII

CLASSES OF PRONOUNS

I. PERSONAL PRONOUNS

Point out the pronouns in the following sentences, and tell which denote the person speaking, which the person spoken to, and which the person or thing spoken of : —

1. I am monarch of all I survey.
2. You will be surprised when you read the report.
3. He requested that we should be present.
4. Buy the truth, and sell it not.

A pronoun that shows by its form whether it denotes the person speaking, the person spoken to, or the person or thing spoken of, is a **personal pronoun.**

A pronoun that denotes the person speaking is in the **first person**; as, *I, we.*

A pronoun that denotes a person spoken to is in the **second person**; as, *thou, ye, you.*

A pronoun that denotes a person or a thing spoken of is in the **third person**; as, *he, she, it, they.*

Person is that distinction of pronouns which denotes the speaker, the person spoken to, or the person or thing spoken of.

Nouns have no forms to distinguish person; but a noun is sometimes said to be of the first person when it is in apposition[1] with a pronoun of the first person, and of the second person when it is in apposition with a pronoun of the second person, or when it is used in address; as, —

> 'Tis I, *Hamlet* the Dane. (First person.)
> Thou, *Lord*, seest me. (Second person.)
> O *death*, where is thy sting? (Second person.)

DECLENSION OF THE PERSONAL PRONOUNS

FIRST PERSON

	SINGULAR		PLURAL
Nom.	I	*Nom.*	we
Poss.	my, mine	*Poss.*	our, ours
Obj.	me	*Obj.*	us

The plural form *we* (*our, ours, us*) is sometimes used vaguely for people in general; as, —

> The world is too much with *us;* late and soon,
> Getting and spending, *we* lay waste our powers.
> — WORDSWORTH.

The form *we* is frequently used by editors and authors, when referring to themselves; as, —

> *We* have remarked elsewhere on this portrait.

We is also used by kings and some other rulers in issuing proclamations and giving orders; as, —

> You have good leave to leave *us:* when *we* need
> Your use and counsel, *we* shall send for you.
> — SHAKESPEARE, *Henry IV.*

[1] See page 183.

SECOND PERSON

	SINGULAR		PLURAL
Nom.	thou	*Nom.*	ye, you
Poss.	thy, thine	*Poss.*	your, yours
Obj.	thee	*Obj.*	you

Thou, the second person singular, is no longer in common use. It is now chiefly used in prayer and in poetry; as, —

> Withhold not *thou thy* tender mercies from me.

> I see in *thy* gentle eyes a tear;
>   They turn to me in sorrowful thought;
> *Thou* thinkest of friends, the good and dear,
>   Who were for a time, and now are not. — BRYANT.

The pronoun *you* is used, in ordinary speech, in the place of *thou*, whether one or more than one person is addressed. It is plural in form, and takes a plural verb; as, —

> *You* are merry, my lord. — SHAKESPEARE.
> *You* are not wood, *you* are not stones, but men. — SHAKESPEARE.

THIRD PERSON

| | SINGULAR | | | PLURAL |
	Masc.	*Fem.*	*Neut.*	*Masc., Fem., or Neut.*
Nom.	he	she	it	they
Poss.	his	her, hers	its	their, theirs
Obj.	him	her	it	them

The pronoun of the masculine gender is generally used to refer to a noun which may denote a person of either sex; as, —

> Each pupil must provide *his* own material.

The pronoun of the masculine gender is also used in referring to animals or things that are supposed to possess masculine qualities, and the pronoun of the feminine gender is used in referring to animals or things to which feminine qualities are attributed; as, —

The *eagle* soars above *his* nest.
Earth, with *her* thousand voices, praises God. — COLERIDGE.

The pronoun of the neuter gender is often used to refer to animals or to young children, in cases where the sex is not considered; as, —

The deer raised *its* head.
The infant knew *its* name.

The pronoun *it* is also used as the grammatical subject of a verb which is followed by the real or logical subject; as, —

It is useless to deny the fact.

It is used as an impersonal subject when the meaning intended is expressed or implied by the verb itself; as, —

It rains.   *It* snows.

It is sometimes used as an impersonal or indefinite object; as, —

Come and trip *it* as you go.
They lord *it* over us.

The possessive forms *my*, *thy*, *her*, *our*, *your*, and *their* are used before the nouns they modify, and the forms *mine*, *thine*, *hers*, *ours*, *yours*, and *theirs* are used after the noun; as, —

My sister, but sister *mine*.
This is *my* book.   The book is *mine*.

The possessive forms of the pronoun are often called possessive adjectives.

Mine and *thine* were formerly used before their nouns, provided the nouns began with a vowel sound; as, —

Bow down *thine* ear. I will lift up *mine* eyes unto the hills.

This usage may still be observed in our English Bible and in poetry.

EXERCISE 61

In the following sentences, explain the special uses of the italicized pronouns: —

1. Every member is expected to do *his* part.
2. The child closed *its* eyes.
3. The camel kneels to receive *its* burden.
4.   How glorious, through *his* depths of light,
           Rolls the majestic sun!
5. The deer left *her* delicate footprint in the soft mould.
6. The bear broke away from *his* keeper.
7.   The sea is mighty, but a mightier sways
           His restless billows.
8.   The merry lark, he soars on high,
           No worldly thought o'ertakes *him;*
         He sings aloud to the clear blue sky,
           And the daylight that awakes him.
         As sweet a lay, as loud, as gay,
           The nightingale is trilling;
         With feeling bliss, no less than his,
           Her little heart is thrilling. — HARTLEY COLERIDGE.
9. *It* is one thing to be well informed, *it* is another to be wise.
10. Thy mistress leads thee a dog's life of *it.*

11. *It* is said that he will speak.

12. They had to foot *it* to the station.

13. Agree with *thine* adversary quickly.

14. And now there came both mist and snow,
     And *it* grew wondrous cold. — COLERIDGE.

CHAPTER XXIX

COMPOUND PERSONAL PRONOUNS

Tell how the italicized pronouns in the following sentences are formed, and how each is used : —

1. The boy hurt *himself*.
2. We often deceive *ourselves*.
3. I *myself* heard the remark.

The pronouns *my*, *our*, *thy*, *your*, *him*, *her*, *it*, and *them* are used with *self* or *selves* to form **compound personal pronouns**; thus, —

COMPOUND PERSONAL PRONOUNS

	SINGULAR	PLURAL
First Person.	myself	ourselves
Second Person.	{ thyself yourself	yourselves
Third Person.	{ himself herself itself	themselves

The compound personal pronouns are used for **emphasis** in the nominative and the objective, either in apposition with a noun or pronoun or alone ; as, —

I *myself* longed to go.

Then rest thee here till dawn of day;
Myself will guide thee on thy way. —SCOTT.

Here we met the poet *himself*.

The compound personal pronouns are also used in the objective case as **reflexives**, that is, as objects denoting the same person or thing as the subject of the verb; as, —

He hid *himself* from his friends.
I let *myself* down with a rope.

Formerly the simple personal pronoun was used reflexively; as, —

Now I lay *me* down to sleep.

This usage is now rare, except as an indirect object; as, —

I have bought *me* a new hat.

EXERCISE 62

Tell which pronouns in the following sentences are used emphatically and which reflexively : —

1. A house divided against itself cannot stand.
2. He himself was not the author of the article.
3. We found ourselves in an absolutely French region.
4. He bowed to the audience and then seated himself.
5. The book itself could hardly be called a novel.
6. They interested themselves in the sports of the children.
7. I myself longed to cut free from prescribed bondage.
8. Thus influenced, I conquered myself in a single evening, and lost my shyness forever.
9. These remarks helped me to justify to myself that early choice.

CHAPTER XXX

CLASSES OF PRONOUNS— *Continued*

II. ADJECTIVE PRONOUNS

Which of the italicized words below are used as adjectives? Which are used as pronouns?

1. *Many* tickets were sold.
2. *Many* were unable to secure seats.
3. Look at *this* clock.
4. *This* is sold.

Certain words can be used to limit nouns or to stand for nouns. When such words limit nouns, they are adjectives; when they stand for nouns they are **adjective pronouns.** Sometimes there is a difference of form; as, *no* (adj.), *none* (pro.); *other* (adj.), *others* (pro.).

Adjective pronouns are sometimes divided into the following classes : —

(1) **Demonstrative pronouns,** those pointing out the things to which they relate ; as, *this* (plural *these*), *that* (plural *those*).

(2) **Distributive pronouns,** those relating to persons or things considered separately ; as, *each, either, neither.*

(3) **Reciprocal pronouns,** those expressing a mutual or reciprocal relation ; as, *each other, one another.*

They feared *each other* (that is, *each* feared the *other*).

They assisted *one another* (that is, *each* one of them assisted *another*).

(4) **Indefinite pronouns,** those not specifying any particular individual or thing; as, *all, another, any, both, few, many, none, one, other, several, some.*

Some adjective pronouns are inflected for number and case. Thus, *this* and *that* have the plural forms *these* and *those; one* and *other* have plural and possessive forms; and *either* and *another* have a form for the possessive singular.

EXERCISE 63

Tell whether the italicized words in the following sentences are adjectives or pronouns, giving reasons in each case : —

1. *Many,* alas ! had fallen in battle. — HAWTHORNE.

2. There is a calm for *those* who weep. — J. MONTGOMERY.

3.   *All* are architects of fate,
          Working in *these* walls of time ;
      Some with massive deeds and great,
          Some with ornaments of rhyme. — LONGFELLOW.

4. *Any* life that is worth living must be a struggle.
                         — DEAN STANLEY.

5. The man deserving the name is *one* whose thoughts and exertions are for *others* rather than for himself. — SIR WALTER SCOTT.

6. *All* men think *all* men mortal but themselves. — YOUNG.

7. Men at *some* time are masters of their fate. — SHAKESPEARE.

8. *This* was the noblest Roman of them all. — SHAKESPEARE.

9. My worthy friend Sir Roger is *one* of *those* who is not only at peace with himself, but beloved and esteemed by *all* about him.
                         — ADDISON.

10. It is *one* thing to be well informed ; it is *another* to be wise. — ROBERTSON.

11. We too seldom think how much we owe to *those* formidable savages. — JOHN FISKE.

12. *Few* shall part where *many* meet. — CAMPBELL.

13.   To know
                 That which before us lies in daily life
                 Is the prime wisdom. — MILTON.

EXERCISE 64

Construct sentences containing the following words used (1) *as adjectives;* (2) *as pronouns:* —

both	each	few	several	these
neither	none	many	that	other

CHAPTER XXXI

CLASSES OF PRONOUNS — *Continued*

III. RELATIVE PRONOUNS

Tell how many assertions are made in each of the following sentences, read the principal statement, and state the office of the italicized part: —

1. We found a guide, *who answered our questions.*
2. The wind, *which rose suddenly*, had now ceased.
3. They *that seek wisdom* will be wise.

Which words in the dependent clauses above refer to preceding nouns, and how are the dependent clauses joined to the independent clauses?

A pronoun that refers or relates to a noun or another pronoun, and joins to it a dependent clause, is a **relative pronoun.**

The noun or pronoun to which a relative pronoun refers or relates is called its **antecedent,** because the antecedent usually precedes the pronoun; as, —

What is that *sound which* now bursts on his ear?

He who would be great in the eyes of others must first learn to be nothing in his own.

The simple relative pronouns are *who, which, that,* and *what.*

EXERCISE 65

Point out the relative pronouns in the following sentences, name their antecedents, and tell what the pronouns connect: —

1. This was a signal to the patriots, who instantly despatched swift messengers to rouse the country.

2. We made preparations for our journey, which lay through mountainous regions.

3. They were accompanied by some Indians, who were skilful divers.

4. They saw nothing more valuable than a curious sea-shrub, which was growing beneath the water.

5.
       He that filches from me my good name
       Robs me of that which not enriches him,
       And makes me poor indeed. —SHAKESPEARE.

6. In the centre of the wood stood an enormous tulip tree, which towered like a giant above all the other trees of the neighborhood.

7. The general, who was on horseback, ordered the troops to halt.

8. They have taken forts that military men said could not be taken.

9. They that have done this deed are honorable.

The flame that lit the battle's wreck
Shone round him o'er the dead.

11. Is it the wind that moaneth bleak?

12. It is indeed impossible to kill a weed, which the soil has a natural disposition to produce.

CHAPTER XXXII

USE OF RELATIVE PRONOUNS

Who is usually applied to persons; as, —

Hail to the chief *who* in triumph advances. — SCOTT.

Old Kasper took it from the boy,
   Who stood expectant by. — SOUTHEY.

Can this be she,
The lady, *who* knelt at the old oak tree? — COLERIDGE.

Sometimes, particularly in the description of individual traits or acts, *who* refers to animals; as, —

Twice have the crow-blackbirds attempted a settlement in my pines, and twice have the robins, *who* claim a right of preëmption, so successfully played the part of border-ruffians as to drive them away. — LOWELL.

In the next cage [we see] a hyena from Africa, *who* has doubtless howled around the pyramids. — HAWTHORNE.

I knew a tame deer in a settlement in the edge of the forest, *who* had the misfortune to break her leg. — C. D. WARNER.

He was only answered by the cawing of a flock of idle crows, . . . *who*, secure in their elevation, seemed to look down and scoff at the poor man's perplexities. — IRVING.

Which is applied to the lower animals and to things without life ; as, —

His good steed, *which* had borne him through many a hard fight, had fallen under him. — PRESCOTT.

Nature has indeed given us a soil *which* yields bounteously to the hands of industry. — WEBSTER.

Which was formerly used in speaking of persons ; as, —

Our Father *which* art in heaven.

Which sometimes has a phrase or a clause for its antecedent ; as, —

In the midst of these my musings she desired me to reach her a little salt upon the point of my knife, *which* I did in such a trepidation and hurry of obedience that I let it drop by the way.

— ADDISON.

It is probable that when this great work was begun, *which* must have been many hundred years ago, there was religion among this people. — ADDISON.

As he approached the village, he met a number of people, but none whom he knew, *which* somewhat surprised him, for he had thought himself acquainted with every one in the country round.

— IRVING.

When he was angered, *which* was often enough, he gave his commands and breathed threats of punishment like any king.

— R. L. STEVENSON.

In each of the foregoing examples, *which* refers not to a single word, but to the idea expressed by the preceding clause.

That is applied to persons, to animals, and to things; as, —

Thrice is he armed *that* hath his quarrel just. — SHAKESPEARE.

Even the very dog *that* lay stretched at his feet . . . would look fondly up in his master's face. — IRVING.

A city *that* is set on a hill cannot be hid. — BIBLE.

That is generally preferred to *who* or *which* —

(1) In introducing a relative clause that limits or restricts the meaning of the antecedent;[1] as, —

> They *that* touch pitch will be defiled.

(2) After a joint reference to persons and things; as, —

> Where are the boy and dog *that* we met?

When the relative *that* is used as the object of a preposition, the preposition follows the pronoun; as, —

> Here is the hat *that* you looked *at*.

What refers to things. It is generally used without an antecedent expressed, and is equivalent to *that which;* as, —

> She remembers *what* (that which) she reads.

As is sometimes used as a relative pronoun. It is then usually preceded by *such;* as, —

> Let such *as* (those who) hear take heed.

---

[1] Some recent authorities teach that only *that* should be used when the relative clause is limiting or defining; as, the man *that* runs fastest wins the race; but *who* or *which* when it is descriptive or coördinating: as, this man, *who* ran fastest, won the race; but, though present usage is perhaps tending in the direction of such a distinction, it neither has been nor is a rule of English speech, nor is it likely to become one. — THE CENTURY DICTIONARY.

But is sometimes a relative pronoun. It has a negative force; as, —

> There is no fireside, howsoe'er defended,
> *But* has (*that* has *not*) one vacant chair. — LONGFELLOW.

DECLENSION OF RELATIVE PRONOUNS

Who is declined, in both singular and plural, with the nominative *who*, the possessive *whose*, and the objective *whom*; as, —

> Blessed is he *who* has found his work.
> There is a reaper *whose* name is Death.
> He *whom* I loved is dead.

The other relative pronouns are not declined, but *whose* is often used as if it were the possessive form of *which* (that is, as equivalent to *of which*); as, —

> Bordered with trees *whose* gay leaves fly. — BRYANT.

The simple relative pronouns have the following forms: —

SINGULAR AND PLURAL

Nom.	who	which	that	what
Poss.	whose	(whose)	——	——
Obj.	whom	which	that	what

COMPOUND RELATIVE PRONOUNS

Pronouns formed by adding *ever*, *so*, or *soever* to *who*, *which*, and *what* are called **compound relative pronouns**; as, *whoever*, *whoso*, *whosoever*; *whichever*, *whichsoever*; *whatever*, *whatsoever*.

These compounds are generally used without antecedents expressed. Thus, —

> *Whoever* looks may find the spot.
> *Whoso* diggeth a pit shall fall therein.
> *Whosoever* will save his life, shall lose it.
> *Whatsoever* thy hand findeth to do, do it with thy might.

Since they do not refer to definite persons. or things, they are sometimes called **indefinite relative pronouns**.

Whoever and *whosoever* are declined as follows : —

SINGULAR AND PLURAL

Nom.	whoever	whosoever
Poss.	whosever	whosesoever
Obj.	whomever	whomsoever

The person, number, and gender of a relative pronoun are determined by its antecedent, thus : —

> He prayeth best, *who* loveth best
> All things, both great and small. —COLERIDGE.

In this example, *who* refers to *he*, hence it is third person, singular number, and masculine gender.

The case of a relative pronoun depends upon its use in its own clause. Thus, in the sentence, "Uneasy lies the head *that* wears a crown," *that* is the subject of the verb *wears*, hence it is in the nominative case. In the sentence, "The evil *that* men do lives after them," *that* is the object of the verb *do*, and is, therefore, in the objective case.

EXERCISE 66

Point out the relative pronouns in the following sentences, name their antecedents, tell what the pronouns connect, and give the person, number, gender, and case of each: —

1. He that lacks time to mourn lacks time to mend.

2. Where lies the land to which the ship would go?

3. My ramble soon led me to the church, which stood a little distance from the village.— IRVING.

4. What a man has learnt is of importance, but what he is, what he can do, what he will become, are more significant things.

— HELPS.

5. He that is slow to anger is better than the mighty.— BIBLE.

6. A land that will not yield satisfactorily without irrigation, and whose best paying produce requires intelligent as well as careful husbandry, will never be an idle land. — WARNER.

7.   All precious things, discovered late,
    To those that seek them issue forth. — TENNYSON.

8.   They are slaves who dare not be
    In the right with two or three.— LOWELL.

9. Here, then, I parted, sorrowfully, from the companion with whom I set out on my journey.— HOLMES.

10. He who has sought renown about the world, and has reaped a full harvest of worldly favor, will find, after all, that there is no love, no admiration, no applause, so sweet to the soul as that which springs up in his native place. — IRVING.

11. We have no bird whose song will match the nightingale's in compass, none whose note is so rich as that of the European blackbird : but for mere rapture I have never heard the bobo-link's rival. — LOWELL.

12. Whoever examines the maps of London which were published toward the close of the reign of Charles the Second will see that only the nucleus of the present capital then existed.

— MACAULAY.

13. Whatever befell them, it was not dishonor, and whatever failed them, they were not found wanting to themselves.

—R. L. STEVENSON.

14. Whatsoever he doeth shall prosper.

15. The books which help you most are those which make you think most. — PARKER.

16. They never fail who die in a great cause. — BYRON.

17. The Upper Lake discharges itself into the Lower by a brook which winds through a mile and a half of swamp and woods. — WARNER.

18. I tell you that which you yourselves do know.

— SHAKESPEARE.

19. How beautiful upon the mountains are the feet of him that bringeth good tidings ! — BIBLE.

20. Where are the flowers, the fair young flowers, that lately
    sprang and stood
  In brighter light, and softer air, a beauteous sisterhood?

21.   The charities that soothe and heal and bless,
    Lie scattered at the feet of men like flowers.

22.   There breathes not clansman of thy line
    But would have given his life for mine. — SCOTT.

OMISSION OF THE RELATIVE PRONOUN

The relative pronoun is often omitted when, if expressed, it would be in the objective case; as, —

Observe the language well in all [*that*] you write.

In poetry, the relative pronoun is sometimes omitted, even when it would be the subject; as, —

'Tis distance [*that*] lends enchantment to the view. — CAMPBELL.

The antecedent of a relative pronoun is sometimes omitted, being implied in the pronoun; as, —

[*He*] Who breaks, pays.

EXERCISE 67

Tell where relative pronouns are omitted in the following sentences, and name the case of each omitted word: —

1. I am not altogether unqualified for the business I have undertaken. — ADDISON.
2. All the faces he drew were very remarkable for their smiles.
— ADDISON.

3. The house we lived in is sold.
4. Few and short were the prayers we said. — WOLFE.

5. The stranger at my fireside cannot see
The forms I see, nor hear the sounds I hear. — LONGFELLOW.

6. 'Tis the sunset of life gives me mystical lore. — CAMPBELL.
7. I am monarch of all I survey. — COWPER.
8. Nearly all of his poems were intended to further a cause he held dear, or to teach a lesson he thought needful.

9. All I hear
Is the north wind drear.

CHAPTER XXXIII

RELATIVE CLAUSES

EXPLANATORY AND RESTRICTIVE

Tell which clauses, in the following sentences, introduce additional ideas about the antecedents, and which limit or restrict their meaning : —

1. The physician, who was in the next room, entered.

2.   I thrice presented him a kingly crown,
      Which he did thrice refuse.

3. I know the man that must hear me.

4. They that have done this deed are honorable.

A clause that introduces an additional idea about the antecedent is **explanatory** ; as, —

They had one son, who had grown up to be the staff and pride of their age.

The cargo, which was valuable, was lost.

A clause that limits or restricts the meaning of the antecedent is **restrictive** ; as, —

      The bird *that soars on highest wing*
      Builds on the ground her lowly nest.

That is generally preferred to *who* or *which* in introducing a restrictive clause.[1]

A relative clause not restrictive is separated from the remainder of the sentence by the comma.

---

[1] See footnote, page 70.

EXERCISE 68

Point out the relative pronouns in the following sentences, and tell in each case whether they introduce explanatory or restrictive clauses : —

1. He that is not with me is against me.

2. The Carrier, who had turned his face from the door, signed to him to go if he would. — DICKENS.

3. Carefully then were covered the embers that glowed on the hearthstone. — LONGFELLOW.

4. Not far from the gateway they came to a bridge, which seemed to be built of iron. — HAWTHORNE.

5. The first spring wild-flowers, whose shy faces among the dry leaves and rocks are so welcome, yield no honey. — JOHN BURROUGHS.

6. The tongue is like a race-horse, which runs the faster the less weight it carries. — ADDISON.

7. We were the first that ever burst
     Into that silent sea. — COLERIDGE.

8. Bordered with trees whose gay leaves fly
     On every breath that sweeps the sky
     The fresh dark acres furrowed lie,
       And ask the sower's hand. — BRYANT.

9. The mind that lies fallow but a single day sprouts up in follies that are only to be killed by a constant and assiduous culture. — ADDISON.

10. A tree, which grew out from the hillside, was the living centre-beam of the roof. — STEVENSON.

11. And everybody praised the Duke,
      Who this great fight did win. — SOUTHEY.

12. Brazil, which is nearly as large as the whole of Europe, is covered with a vegetation of incredible profusion. Indeed, so rank and luxuriant is the growth, that Nature seems to riot in the very wantonness of power. A great part of this immense country is filled with dense and tangled forests, whose noble trees, blossoming in unrivalled beauty, and exquisite with a thousand hues, throw out their produce in endless prodigality. On their summit are perched birds of gorgeous plumage, which nestle in their dark and lofty recesses. Below, their bases and trunks are crowded with brushwood, creeping plants, innumerable parasites, all swarming with life. There, too, are myriads of insects of every variety; reptiles of strange and singular form; serpents and lizards, spotted with deadly beauty: all of which find means of existence in this vast workshop and repository of Nature. And that nothing may be wanting to this land of marvels, the forests are skirted by enormous meadows, which, reeking with heat and moisture, supply nourishment to countless herds of wild cattle, that browse and fatten on their herbage; while the adjoining plains, rich in another form of life, are the chosen abode of the subtlest and most ferocious animals, which prey on each other, but which it almost seems no human power can hope to extirpate. — BUCKLE.

EXERCISE 69

Select from your Reader or History six relative clauses that are explanatory, and six others that are restrictive.

CHAPTER XXXIV

CLASSES OF PRONOUNS—*Continued*

IV. INTERROGATIVE PRONOUNS

How are the italicized words used in the following sentences?

1. *Who* comes here?
2. *Which* reached home first?
3. *What* is the news?

A pronoun used in asking a question is an **interrogative pronoun**. An interrogative pronoun may be used in a direct or an indirect question; thus, —

> *What* did you see? (Direct question.)
> I asked *what* you saw. (Indirect question.)

The interrogative pronouns are *who*, *which*, and *what*.

Who refers to persons. It is declined like the relative **who**.

Which refers to persons or to things. It implies selection; as, —

> *Which* of the brothers sings?
> *Which* of the chairs do you prefer?

What refers to things; as, —

> *What* was in the box?

Whether was formerly in common use as an interrogative pronoun; as, —

> *Whether* is greater, the gift or the altar?

Which and *what* are sometimes used as **interrogative adjectives**; as, —

> *Which* way shall I fly?
> Where are they now? *What* lands and skies
> Paint pictures in their friendly eyes?
> *What* hope deludes, *what* promise cheers,
> *What* pleasant voices fill their ears? — LONGFELLOW.

As an interrogative adjective, *what*, like *which*, is used of persons as well as of things ; as, —

What man would say such a thing?   *Which* boy replied?

EXERCISE 70

Point out the pronouns in the following sentences, tell the kind of each pronoun, and name its case : —

1. Who can understand his errors ?
2. Which of you, by taking thought, can add one cubit unto his stature ?
3. Shall the clay say to him that fashioneth it, What makest thou?
4. Who planted this old apple tree?
5. What is civilization?   What does it consist in?
6. Whom shall I send?
7. Ah ! what is that sound which now bursts on his ear? — DIMOND.
8. Who, among the whole chattering crowd, can tell me of the forms and the precipices of the chain of tall white mountains that girded the horizon at noon yesterday?   Who saw the narrow sunbeam that came out of the south, and smote upon their summits until they melted and mouldered away in a dust of blue rain?   Who saw the dance of the dead clouds when the sunlight left them last night, and the west wind blew them before it like withered leaves? — RUSKIN.

EXERCISE 71

Tell whether the italicized words in the following sentences are interrogative or relative pronouns, giving a reason in each instance : —

1. *What* is the Constitution?   It is the bond *which* binds together millions of brothers. — DANIEL WEBSTER.

2. The divine faculty is to see *what* everybody can look at.—
—Lowell.

3.   Now tell us all about the war,
        And *what* they fought each other for. —Southey.

4.   The lovely lady Christabel,
        Whom her father loves so well,
        What makes her in the wood so late,
        A furlong from the castle gate? — Coleridge.

5. It was with great difficulty that the self-important man in the cocked hat restored order ; and having assumed a tenfold austerity of brow, demanded again of the unknown culprit, *what* he came there for, and *whom* he was seeking. — Irving.

6. Do you ask *what* the birds say ?

7. Things are not *what* they seem.

8. *Who* is the great man ? He *who* is the strongest in the exercise of patience ; he *who* patiently endures injury.

CHAPTER XXXV

HOW TO PARSE PRONOUNS

To parse a pronoun, state —

(1) Its **class.**
(2) Its **antecedent** (if it is a relative pronoun).
(3) Its **person** (if it is a personal or a relative pronoun).
(4) Its **number.**
(5) Its **gender** (if it is a personal pronoun of the third person singular).
(6) Its **case.**
(7) Its **syntax** or **construction** — use in the sentence.

EXAMPLE I. And then *I* think of *one who* in *her* youthful beauty died.

1. *I* is a personal pronoun, first person, singular number, and nominative case — subject of the verb *think*.[1]

2. *One* is an adjective pronoun, third person, singular number, and objective case — object of the preposition *of*.

3. *Who* is a relative pronoun, third person, singular number, agreeing with its antecedent *one*, and nominative case — subject of the verb *died*.

4. *Her* is a personal pronoun, third person, singular number, feminine gender, and possessive case — depending upon the noun *beauty*.

EXAMPLE II. No one heard what he said.

What is a relative pronoun, used without an antecedent expressed, of the third person, singular number, and objective case — object of the verb *said*.

EXERCISE 72

Parse the pronouns in the following sentences : —

1. The moon did not rise till after ten, so I had two hours of intense darkness during which I used my ears instead of my eyes.
— M. THOMPSON.

2. And what is so rare as a day in June? — LOWELL.

3. Hang around your walls pictures which shall tell stories of mercy, hope, courage, faith, and charity. — D. G. MITCHELL.

4. A few hoped, and many feared, that some scheme of monarchy would be established. — JOHN FISKE.

---

[1] Or follow a briefer form, similar to the one suggested on p. 54.

5.
> With merry songs we mock the wind
> That in the pine top grieves,
> And slumber long and sweetly
> On beds of oaken leaves. — BRYANT.

6. I witnessed a striking incident in bird life which was very suggestive. — M. THOMPSON.

7. Hast thou a charm to stay the morning star? — COLERIDGE.

8. He laid him down and closed his eyes. — SOUTHEY.

9.
> Triumphant arch, that fill'st the sky
> When storms prepare to part,
> I ask not proud Philosophy
> To teach me what thou art. — CAMPBELL.

10.
> He that only rules by terror
> Doeth grievous wrong. — TENNYSON.

11. We judge ourselves by what we feel capable of doing, while others judge us by what we have already done. — LONGFELLOW.

12.
> I fear thee, ancient mariner!
> I fear thy skinny hand!
> And thou art long, and lank, and brown,
> As is the ribbed sea-sand. — COLERIDGE.

13. Some are born great, some achieve greatness, and some have greatness thrust upon them. — SHAKESPEARE.

14. He who plants an oak looks forward to future ages, and plants for posterity. — IRVING.

15. Which of us shall be the soonest folded to that dim Unknown?
> Which shall leave the other walking in this flinty path alone? — BRYANT.

CHAPTER XXXVI

REVIEW OF PRONOUNS

EXERCISE 73

What is a pronoun? How does a pronoun differ from a noun?

Mention the different classes of pronouns and give examples of each class.

What is a personal pronoun? How many case forms has the pronoun of the first person? How is each used?

Give the second person singular, and tell how it is used. Give two uses of the pronoun *you*.

Which person has a distinction of gender? State special uses of the pronouns of the masculine, feminine, and neuter genders. How are the possessive forms of personal pronouns used?

Mention the compound personal pronouns, and tell how they are formed.

Give an example of their use as *reflexives;* for *emphasis*. How does an adjective pronoun differ from an adjective?

Define a relative pronoun. State the distinctions in the use of *who*, *which*, and *what*. Give a sentence in which *as* is used as a relative pronoun; in which *but* is so used.

What is an interrogative pronoun? What words are used as interrogative pronouns?

CHAPTER XXXVII

CLASSES OF ADJECTIVES

Point out the adjectives in the following sentences, and tell what each expresses: —

1. I bring fresh showers for the thirsting flowers.
2. The sun is warm, the sky is clear.
3. A little leaven leaveneth the whole lump.
4. Three years she grew in sun and shower.

(1) An adjective that expresses quality or kind is a **descriptive adjective**; as, a *happy* boy; a *narrow* path; a *wooden* bench.

The following terms are sometimes applied to certain descriptive adjectives: —

(*a*) **Proper Adjectives,** those formed from proper names; as, *American* forests; the *English* language. Proper adjectives begin with capital letters.

(*b*) **Participial Adjectives,** which are participles[1] used simply as adjectives; as, *burning* words, the *rising* sun, *withered* leaves.

(2) An adjective that points out something or denotes number or quantity is a **limiting adjective**; as, *this* week; *two* hours; *much* trouble.

A limiting adjective may be used —

(*a*) Simply to point out; as, *this, that, the, an, yon, yonder.* Such **adjectives** are sometimes called **demonstrative adjectives.**

[1] See page 115.

(*b*) To express a definite number; as, *one, two, fourteen, fifty*.

(*c*) To express an indefinite number or quantity; as, *any, little, much, many, some*.

(*d*) To show the order of things in a series; as, *first, second, third*.

Limiting adjectives expressing number are called **numeral adjectives**. Numerals are classified as —

(*a*) **Cardinals**, those denoting how many; as, *one, two, three*.

(*b*) **Ordinals**, those denoting the order of things in a series; as, *third, fourth, fifth*.

An adjective formed from two simple words is called a **compound adjective**; as, *native-born* citizen, *rock-bound* coast, *low-vaulted* roof, *twenty-third* psalm.

EXERCISE 74

Point out the adjectives in the following sentences, state the office of each, and tell what kind of adjective it is : —

1. Thirty-two statues of various sizes were found in this field.
2. Its chief attractions were a never-failing breeze at night, good water, and a large garden in the centre of a cleared space.
3. Hark ! 'tis the twanging horn o'er yonder bridge.— COWPER.
4. We met several men riding at a rapid pace.

5. Across its antique portico
     Tall poplar-trees their shadows throw.— LONGFELLOW.

6. This long march through the primeval forest and over rugged and trackless mountains was one of the most remarkable exploits of the war.

7. O blessings on his kindly voice and on his silver hair!
8. Suddenly there was a gentle little tap on the inside of the lid.
9. The thirteen colonies were now free and independent states.
10. A certain man fell among thieves.
11. Small service is true service while it lasts. — WORDSWORTH.
12. All the air a solemn stillness holds. — GRAY.
13. The good old year is with the past. — BRYANT.

14.   With a slow and noiseless footstep
         Comes that messenger divine. — LONGFELLOW.

15.   With fingers weary and worn,
              With eyelids heavy and red,
         A woman sat, in unwomanly rags,
              Plying her needle and thread. — HOOD.

16.   All the little boys and girls,
         With rosy cheeks and flaxen curls,
         And sparkling eyes and teeth like pearls,
         Tripping and skipping, ran merrily after
         The wonderful music with shouting and laughter.
                                             — BROWNING.

EXERCISE 75

Write sentences containing the following words used as adjectives : —

strong	any	many	brittle	prompt
fair	all	curved	every	distant
both	dutiful	little	modern	neither
some	few	much	each	another
clear	brief	certain	other	several

CHAPTER XXXVIII

ARTICLES

The limiting adjectives *the* and *an* or *a* (the shortened form of *an*) are sometimes called **articles**.

The is the weakened form of *that*. It is called the **definite article**.

The is used to point out some particular thing or things or a class of things;[1] as, —

And *the* Piper advanced and *the* children followed. — BROWNING.

The stars are out by twos and threes. — WORDSWORTH.

An or *a* is the weakened form of the numeral adjective *one*. It is called the **indefinite article**.

An or *a* is used to point out any one thing of a class; as, —

A man has no more right to say *an* uncivil thing than to act one. — DR. JOHNSON.

While the indefinite article is generally used before a singular noun, it is also used before a plural noun with *few, great, many,* or *good many;* as, —

A few days, *a great many* books, *a good many* people.

The indefinite article should not be used before a word denoting a whole class. Thus, not "What kind of *a* bird was it?" "I do not like that sort of *a* thing"; but "What kind of bird was it?" "I do not like that sort of thing."

---

[1] In such phrases as "*the* more *the* merrier," *the* is not an article, but an adverb. See page 220.

EXERCISE 76

In the following sentences find the articles that point out
(1) *some particular thing or things;* (2) *a class of things;*
(3) *any one thing of a class:*—

1. Blessed is the man that walketh not in the counsel of the wicked.

2. A wise man will make haste to forgive.

3. The shamrock is the national emblem of Ireland.

4. A fair little girl sat under a tree.

5. The salmon is both a marine and a fresh-water fish.

6. He returned with the title of Admiral.

7.   The maples redden in the sun;
         In autumn gold the beeches stand.

8. Consider the lilies how they grow.

AN OR A

An is used before a word beginning with a vowel sound;[1]
as, *an* apple; *an* initial; *an* hour.

A is used before a word beginning with a consonant
sound; as, *a* boat; *a* day; many *a* one (*one* begins with the
consonant sound of *w*); *a* unit (*unit* begins with the consonant sound of *y*).

EXERCISE 77

*Read the following sentences, supplying the proper form of
the indefinite article. Give in each case a reason for your
choice:*—

1. Be —— hero in the strife.
2. He is —— humorist.

---

[1] *An* was formerly used before all words beginning with *h*, and is still used
by many writers before *h* in unaccented syllables; as, *an* hotel; *an* historian.

3. For Brutus is —— honorable man.

4. He that hath —— trade hath —— estate, and he that hath —— calling hath —— office of profit and honor.

5. Such —— one is seldom found.

6. I learned that he was —— universal favorite in the village.

7. That book is —— authority on this subject.

8.   —— hundred dogs bayed deep and strong,
    Clattered —— hundred steeds along,
    Their peal the merry horns rung out,
    —— hundred voices joined the shout.

9.   The shades of night were falling fast,
    As through —— Alpine village passed
    —— youth, who bore, 'mid snow and ice,
    —— banner with the strange device,
              Excelsior !

10. Truth is the highest thing —— man may keep.

REPETITION OR OMISSION OF THE ARTICLE

When two or more adjectives modify the same noun, the article is used before the first only ; but when they modify different nouns, expressed or understood, the article is used before each ; as, —

> *A* red and white rose (one rose).
> *A* red and *a* white rose (two roses).

Sometimes, however, when the adjectives modify the same noun, the article is repeated for emphasis ; as " *An* amusing and *an* instructive book."

The article is sometimes used before each adjective with a noun in the singular, and before the first adjective only with a noun in the plural; as, "Omit *the* second and *the* third stanza," or "Omit *the* second and third stanzas."

When two or more connected nouns refer to the same person or thing, the article is used before the first only; but when they refer to different persons or things that are to be especially distinguished, the article is used before each; as, —

He was *an* eminent orator and statesman.

Its effect approaches to that produced by *the* pencil or *the* chisel. — MACAULAY.

In expressing a comparison, if two nouns refer to the same person or thing, the article is used before the first noun only; but if they refer to different persons or things, the article must be used with each noun; as, —

1. He would make *a* better statesman than orator (= He would make a better statesman than [he would make an] orator).

2. He would make *a* better statesman than *an* orator (= He would make a better statesman than an orator [would make]).

EXERCISE 78

Give reasons for the repetition or the omission of the article in each of the following sentences: —

1. He purchased from the Indians a large and fertile tract of land.

2. Wanted, a stenographer and typewriter.

3. Wanted, a stenographer and a typewriter.

4. To the wise and good, old age presents a scene of tranquil enjoyment.

5. On the rich and the eloquent, on nobles and priests, they looked down with contempt.

6. Here was a type of the beginning and the end of human pomp and power.

7. He had, indeed, a quick observation and a retentive memory.

8. What manner of man is this, that even the wind and the sea obey him !

9. He detected, with unfailing skill, the good or the vile wherever it existed.

10. However strange, however grotesque, may be the appearance which Dante undertakes to describe, he never shrinks from describing it. He gives us the shape, the color, the sound, the smell, the taste.

11. The third and fourth chapters are brief and dry.

12. Have you read the seventh and the eighth chapter?

13. He is a better speaker than writer.

14. He was a ready orator, an elegant poet, a skilful gardener, an excellent cook, and a most contemptible sovereign.

15. They elected a secretary and a treasurer.

16. He had naturally a generous and feeling heart.

17. Down in a green and shady bed a modest violet grew.

18. What is the difference between a vowel and a consonant?

CHAPTER XXXIX

COMPARISON OF ADJECTIVES

Tell how many forms the adjective *long* has in the following sentences, and what each form expresses : —

1. This work requires a long pencil.
2. Your pencil is longer than mine.
3. Here is the longest pencil in the box.

Some adjectives change their form to express different degrees of quality. This change of form is called **comparison**.

The form of an adjective that simply expresses the quality is the **positive degree**; as, *long, short*.

The form of an adjective that expresses a higher or a lower degree of the quality is the **comparative degree**; as, *longer, shorter*.

The form of an adjective that expresses the highest or the lowest degree of the quality is the **superlative degree**; as, *longest, shortest*.

Most adjectives of one syllable add *er* to the simple form of the adjective, to form the comparative, and *est*, to form the superlative. If the adjective ends in *e*, one *e* is omitted; as, —

POSITIVE	COMPARATIVE	SUPERLATIVE
long	*longer*	*longest*
pure	*purer*	*purest*

In adding these suffixes the usual rules for spelling must be observed. Thus: —

(1) If the adjective ends in *e*, omit the *e* before adding *er* or *est;* as, *wise, wiser, wisest*.

(2) If the adjective ends in *y*, preceded by a consonant, change the *y* into *i;* as, *happy, happier, happiest*.

(3) If the adjective ends in a single consonant, preceded by a single vowel, double the final consonant; as, *thin, thinner, thinnest*.

Most adjectives of more than one syllable prefix *more* or *less* to the simple form of the adjective, to form the comparative, and *most* or *least*, to form the superlative; as, —

POSITIVE	COMPARATIVE	SUPERLATIVE
careful	*more careful*	*most careful*
fortunate	*less fortunate*	*least fortunate*

A few adjectives of two syllables, ending in sounds that unite easily with the sound of *er* or *est*, may be compared by adding *er* or *est;* as, *noble, happy, narrow, tender, pleasant.* The form of comparison that is most pleasing to the ear should be used.

IRREGULAR COMPARISON

Some adjectives are compared irregularly, as follows:—

POSITIVE	COMPARATIVE	SUPERLATIVE
bad, evil, ill	worse	worst
far	farther, further	farthest, furthest
fore	former	foremost, first
good, well	better	best
hind	hinder	hindmost, hindermost
[in]¹	inner	inmost, innermost
late	latter, later	last, latest
little	less, lesser	least
many, much	more	most
near	nearer	nearest, next
nigh	nigher	nighest, next
old	elder, older	eldest, oldest
[out]	outer, utter	outmost, outermost
		utmost, uttermost
[up]	upper	upmost, uppermost

¹ The words in the brackets are adverbs. No corresponding adjectives exist in the positive form.

MEANINGS OF DOUBLE FORMS

Farther and *further* are often used indiscriminately, though *further* is generally preferred in the sense of additional; as, —

> No *further* reasons were given.

Latter and *last* are used in speaking of order in a series; *later* and *latest* refer to time; as, —

> The *last* volume is just published.
> Have you heard the *latest* news?

Lesser is opposed to *greater*; as, —

God made two great lights; the greater light to rule by day, and the *lesser* light to rule by night.

Elder is opposed to *younger*; *older*, to *new*; as, —

> His *elder* son was in the field.
> Our house is *older* than yours.

Outer is opposed to *inner*; *utter* means *complete*, *total*.

> The *outer* wall has fallen.
> The attempt to sail the boat was an *utter* failure.

Adjectives expressing meanings that do not admit of different degrees cannot, if taken in their strict sense, be compared; as, *one*, *this*, *that*, *equal*, *square*, *vertical*, *perfect*, *universal*.

INFLECTION FOR NUMBER

The two adjectives *this* and *that* are inflected for number; thus, —

Singular	Plural
this	these
that	those

EXERCISE 79

(1) Write the comparison of *beautiful, clear, deep, eloquent, famous, heavy, ill, many, little, well.*

(2) State the distinction in meaning between (*a*) *latter* and *later;* (*b*) *elder* and *older*.

(3) Give ten adjectives that cannot be compared.

EXERCISE 80

Point out each adjective in the following sentences, name its degree, and tell what it modifies.

1. Choose the timbers with greatest care. — Longfellow.

2. Of all the old festivals, however, that of Christmas awakens the strongest and most heartfelt associations. — Irving.

3. He who ascends to mountain tops shall find
   The loftiest peaks most wrapt in clouds and snow. — Byron.

4. The edges and corners of the box were carved with most wonderful skill. — Hawthorne.

5. She is more precious than rubies. — Bible.

6. We started immediately after an early luncheon, followed an excellent road all the way, and were back in time for dinner at half-past six.

7. The day was cloudy, and the sea very rough.

8.   Alas ! when evil men are strong,
       No life is good, no pleasure long. — WORDSWORTH.

9. He that is slow to anger is better than the mighty. — BIBLE.

10. The noblest mind the best contentment has. — SPENSER.

11. This was the noblest Roman of them all. — SHAKESPEARE.

12. The greatest man is he who chooses the right with invincible resólution ; who resists the sorest temptations from within and from without ; who bears the heaviest burdens cheerfully ; who is calmest and most fearless under menaces and frowns ; whose reliance on truth, on virtue, on God, is most unfaltering. — CHANNING.

CHAPTER XL

HOW TO PARSE ADJECTIVES

To parse an adjective, tell —

(1) Its **class**.

(2) Its **degree** of comparison (if the adjective can be compared).

(3) Its **syntax** or **construction** — use in the sentence.

EXAMPLE. — *The north* wind is *cold*.

1. *The* is a limiting adjective, modifying the expression *north wind*.

2. *North* is a descriptive adjective, modifying the noun *wind*.

3. *Cold* is a descriptive adjective of the positive degree. It completes the meaning of the verb *is*, and modifies the noun *wind*, limited by *the* and *north*.

EXERCISE 81

Parse the adjectives in the following sentences : —

1. It is the most beautiful shrub that ever sprang out of the earth.

2. Every good tree bringeth forth good fruit, but a corrupt tree bringeth forth evil fruit.

3.   Such pleasures nerve the arm for strife,
            Bring joyous thoughts and golden dreams.

4. This door led into a passage out of which opened four sleeping-rooms.

5. Wide is the gate and broad is the way.

6. In the middle of the eighteenth century there were four New England colonies. — FISKE.

7. Birds of the polar areas of snow and ice are white, those of the tropics are vari-colored and brilliant-hued. — M. THOMPSON.

8. Straight and strong and magnificently plumed, the palms rose to an average height of seventy or eighty feet. — A. B. EDWARDS.

9. Spring is the season when the volume of bird-song poured round the world is incomparably stronger, fuller, and sweeter than at any other. — M. THOMPSON.

10.   Lo ! while we are gazing, in swifter haste
            Stream down the snows till the air is white. — BRYANT.

11. The habit of observation is the habit of clear and decisive gazing. Not by a first casual glance, but by a steady deliberate aim of the eye are the rare and characteristic things discovered.
                                        — JOHN BURROUGHS.

12.   A form more fair, a face more sweet,
            Ne'er hath it been my lot to meet. — WHITTIER.

13. A beautiful form is better than a beautiful face ; a beautiful behavior is better than a beautiful form : it gives a higher pleasure than statues or pictures; it is the finest of the fine arts.

— EMERSON.

CHAPTER XLI

CHOICE OF ADJECTIVES

The adjectives in the following exercises are often misused. Find out from a dictionary their exact meaning, and be careful to use them in their proper sense.

EXERCISE 82

Copy the following sentences, filling the blanks with appropriate words from this list : —

handsome	beautiful	splendid	fine
pretty	lovely	elegant	grand

1. She lived in a —— cottage by the sea.
2. The Viceroy was welcomed by a —— procession.
3. Niagara is a —— cataract.
4. —— feathers make —— birds.
5. Pegasus was a snow-white steed, with —— silvery wings.
6. She was a lady of —— character.
7. The room was filled with —— furniture.
8. The executive mansion is a —— residence.
9. The view from the top of the mountain is ——.
10. The sunset was ——.
11. We had a —— sail on the lake.

EXERCISE 83

Copy the following sentences, inserting the proper word in each blank. Give in each case a reason for your choice :—

I.—*Cunning, Attractive*

1. What an —— little child she was !
2. The fox is a —— animal.
3. The —— boy eluded his pursuers.

II.—*Dumb, Dull, Stupid*

1. I was —— with silence ; I held my peace.
2. The boy was so —— that he could not understand the problem.
3. He was too —— to express any opinion on the subject.
4. Be kind to —— animals.

III.—*Funny, Strange, Odd*

1. The sailor had many —— adventures.
2. His —— remarks set the table in a roar.
3. He was dressed in an —— way.
4. Misery makes —— bedfellows.
5. The speaker amused his audience with —— stories.

IV.—*Healthy, Healthful, Wholesome*

1. A —— body contributes to the health of the mind.
2. Apples are a —— food.
3. —— food makes a —— man.
4. He sought for a —— climate.
5. The captain was a —— man.

V. — *Mad, Angry*

1. Be ye ——, and sin not.
2. A —— dog ran down the street.
3. This unexpected reply made the boy ——.

VI. — *Ugly, Ill-Natured*

1. The man was so —— that few persons would employ him.
2. Hans Andersen wrote "The —— Duckling."
3. It is hard living with an —— person.

To THE TEACHER. — Many excellent examples for similar study may be found in the selections on pages 255-258, 260, 263-265, 267, 269, and 270.

CHAPTER XLII

REVIEW OF ADJECTIVES

EXERCISE 84

Find the adjectives in the following selection, and state the office of each : —

How beautiful is night !
A dewy freshness fills the silent air ;
No mist obscures, nor cloud nor speck nor stain
Breaks the serene of heaven :
In full-orbed glory yonder moon divine
Rolls through the dark blue depths ;
Beneath her steady ray
The desert circle spreads
Like the round ocean girdled with the sky.
How beautiful is night ! — SOUTHEY.

What is an adjective? Into what two classes may adjectives be divided?

Name three adjectives that are used to point out things; two adjectives that express a definite number; two that express an indefinite number; two that express an indefinite quantity; two that indicate order of things in a series.

State the difference in meaning between *the* and *an* or *a*. Distinguish between the use of *an* and *a*, and illustrate by examples.

Name two adjectives that change their form to denote the plural number. Give their plural forms.

What is meant by the comparison of adjectives? What are the three degrees of comparison called? Define each, and give an example.

How is the comparative formed? Give examples. How is the superlative formed? Give examples.

What is meant by irregular comparison? Illustrate.

Mention two adjectives that are compared by means of suffixes; two that are compared by means of adverbs; two that are compared irregularly; and two that are not usually compared.

Give the comparative and superlative forms of *few, heavy, amiable, swift, useful, fierce, mighty, witty, gentle, good, bad, late, little, ill, much, many.*

CHAPTER XLIII

CLASSES OF VERBS

TRANSITIVE AND INTRANSITIVE VERBS

Point out the verb in each of the following sentences, name its subject,[1] and tell which word is used as the object[2] of the verb: —

1. Spiders spin webs.
2. Bees make honey.
3. Who taught them ?

Some verbs, like the examples above, require objects to complete their meaning; other verbs do not require objects.

A verb that requires an object is a *transitive verb*; as, —

Birds *build* nests.   Henry *threw* the ball.

A verb that does not require an object is an *intransitive verb*; as, —

Birds *fly*.   The sun *shines*.

In a few instances the same word may be used as a transitive verb in one sentence, and as an intransitive verb in another; as, —

The wind *blows* the dust.   (Transitive.)
The wind *blows*.   (Intransitive.)

[1] See page 14.   [2] See page 46.

EXERCISE 86

Point out the verbs in the following sentences, and tell in each case whether the verb is transitive or intransitive :—

1. He shrugged his shoulders, shook his head, cast up his eyes, but said nothing.

2. Each takes his seat, and each receives his share.

3. We scatter seeds with careless hand.

4. A tear stood in his bright blue eye.— LONGFELLOW.

5. A rill of water trickles down the cliff.

6. The piper advanced, and the children followed. — BROWNING.

7. A pair of kingfishers dart back and forth across the bay, in flashes of living blue.

8. Do many good works, and speak few vanities.

9. We carved not a line, and we raised not a stone,
   But we left him alone with his glory. — WOLFE.

10. The heavens declare the glory of God, and the firmament showeth his handiwork.

11. The warrior bowed his crested head. — HEMANS.

12. But soon I heard the dash of oars,
    I heard the pilot's cheer.

13. The fair breeze blew, the white foam flew. — COLERIDGE.

14. In the cold moist earth we laid her, when the forests cast the leaf,
    And we wept that one so lovely should have a life so brief.
    — BRYANT.

EXERCISE 87

Write sentences containing the following words used (1) *as transitive verbs;* (2) *as intransitive verbs:* —

learn	write	watch	strike	ride
roll	see	read	fly	sing

CHAPTER XLIV

VERBS OF INCOMPLETE PREDICATION

Which verbs in the following sentences form a predicate alone, and which must be followed by another word to complete their meaning? —

1. I slip, I slide, I gloom, I glance,
   Among my skimming swallows.

2. The sun is warm, the sky is clear.

3. I bring fresh showers for the thirsting flowers.

A verb that requires an additional word or words to complete the predicate is a verb of **incomplete predication.**

When the verb is transitive, the predicate is completed by the object of the action; as, —

War brings *sorrow.*

When the verb is intransitive, the predicate is completed by a word or words describing the subject, and the completing adjunct is called a **complement**; as, —

The sky is *blue.*   The boy was an orphan.

Most intransitive verbs have a complete meaning in themselves; as, —

The rain *falls*.   The wind *blows*.

A few intransitive verbs (as *be, become, appear, look, seem,* and the like) must be followed by a noun or an adjective to complete their meaning; as, —

He *is* a *statesman*.   The child *seems cold*.

Such verbs of incomplete predication are sometimes called **copulative,** since they connect or couple the subject with a word describing the subject; as, —

Washington *was* a patriot.   She *looks* happy.

EXERCISE 88

Tell whether the verbs in the following sentences are transitive or intransitive, name the object of each transitive verb, and tell what completes the meaning of each incomplete intransitive verb : —

1. He crept softly to the window.
2. The way was long, the wind was cold. — SCOTT.
3.   I heard the bells on Christmas Day
            Their old, familiar carols play. — LONGFELLOW.
4. A thing of beauty is a joy forever. — KEATS.
5. The daffodil is our doorside queen. — BRYANT.
6. The next day Congress took the formal vote upon the resolution.
7. Behold the fowls of the air. — BIBLE.

8.   The fish swam by the castle wall,
            And they seemed joyous, each and all. — BYRON.

9. Open then I flung the shutter, when, with many a flirt and
        flutter,
    In there stepped a stately raven of the saintly days of yore.

                                                            — POE.

10.   The snow had begun in the gloaming,
                And busily all the night
            Had been heaping field and highway
                With a silence deep and white. — LOWELL.

EXERCISE 89

Write (1) *five sentences, each containing a verb of incomplete predication completed by a noun;* (2) *five sentences, each containing a verb of incomplete predication completed by an adjective.*

CHAPTER XLV

ACTIVE AND PASSIVE VOICE

Tell in how many ways each thought is expressed in the following sentences : —

    1. The governor signed the bill.
    2. The bill was signed by the governor.
    3. A hound chased the deer.
    4. The deer was chased by a hound.

A transitive verb may represent its subject as acting or as being acted upon.

A **transitive verb** that represents its subject as acting is said to be in the *active voice;* as, Columbus *discovered* America.

A **transitive verb** that represents its subject as being acted upon is said to be in the *passive voice;* as, America *was discovered* by Columbus.

The object of the verb in the active form becomes the subject of the verb in the passive form. The active voice makes the agent prominent, while the passive voice makes the receiver of the action prominent.

Some verbs usually intransitive become transitive by means of a preposition, and take the passive voice; as, —

> He *laughed at* them.
> They *were laughed* at.

EXERCISE 90

Point out the transitive verbs in the following sentences, and tell the voice of each, giving in each case a reason for your statement : —

1. The frightened animal sought the open country.

2. Our guide had never visited the cave.

3. The building was destroyed by fire, but some of the furniture was saved.

4. The guest was admitted into the parlor.

5. The portrait attracted his notice at once.

6. The petition was signed by a number of prominent citizens.

7. He holds him with his glittering eye. -- COLERIDGE.

8. Many interesting discoveries were made among these broken cliffs. — HAWTHORNE.

9. Here the canoe was driven upon the beach, and the whole party landed.

10. The farmer swung the scythe or turned the hay,
    And 'twixt the heavy swaths his children were at play.
    —BRYANT.

11. On Christmas eve the bells were rung.—SCOTT.

12. The schoolmaster swept and smoothed the ground before the door, trimmed the long grass, trained the ivy and creeping plants which hung their drooping heads in melancholy neglect; and gave to the outer walls a cheery air of home.—DICKENS.

13. A little fire is quickly trodden out.

14. The great iron gateway that opened into the court-yard was locked.

15. Nothing interrupted the stillness of the scene.

CHAPTER XLVI

MODE

Find in the following sentences a verb that asserts something as a fact, one that asserts something as merely thought of or conceived, and one that expresses a command:—

1. He speaks distinctly.
2. If thine enemy *be* hungry, give him bread to eat.
3. Speak the truth.

The manner of asserting is called the **mode** of the verb.

A verb that asserts a thing as a fact or asks a direct question is in the *indicative mode*; as,—

The river *is* deep.
Is the river deep?

A verb that expresses something as conceived rather than as actually true is in the *subjunctive mode ;* as, —

> If he *were* ill, he would inform us.
> Take heed, lest thou *fall*.

A verb in the subjunctive mode is generally preceded by *if*, *though*, *lest*, *unless*, *except*, or some similar word; but these words are not always followed by the subjunctive. When the verb in a conditional clause expresses doubt, it is in the subjunctive mode; but when it expresses probability or certainty it is in the indicative mode; as, —

> If the law *be* unjust, it should be repealed.   (Subjunctive.)
> If the law *is* unjust, let it be repealed.   (Indicative.)

In the first sentence above, doubt is implied about the unjustness of the law; in the second sentence, the unjustness is assumed as a fact.

The most common uses of the subjunctive mode are —

(1) To express a condition or supposition; as, —

> If thou *be* a king, where is thy crown?
> If he *were* here [but he is not], he could explain the matter.

In sentences like the last, the subjunctive expresses a supposition contrary to the actual fact, and refers to present time.

(2) To express a wish; as, —

> O that the day *were* done !

(3) To express purpose; as, —

> Judge not, that ye *be* not judged.
> Watch ye and pray, lest ye *enter* into temptation.

A verb that expresses a command or an entreaty is in the *imperative mode;* as, —

Close the gate.   *Forgive* us our debts.

EXERCISE 91

Tell what each verb expresses in the following sentences, and name its mode : —

1. Consider the lilies of the field.

2.   I stood and watched by the window
           The noiseless work of the sky.

3. I stand upon my native hills again.
4. Thine own friend and thy father's friend, forsake not.
5. Return ye now every one from his evil way.
6. Though this be madness, yet there is method in it.
7. Turn away thine eyes, lest they behold vanity.
8. Though he slay me, yet will I trust him.

EXERCISE 92

Tell the mode of each italicized verb in the following sentences, giving reasons for your statements : —

1. Though your sins *be* as scarlet, they shall be as white as snow.
2. If you *were* in my place, you would think differently.
3. If I *were* hungry, I would not tell thee.
4. Though thou *detain* me, I will not eat of the bread.
5. *Love* not sleep, lest thou *come* to poverty.
6. Thy kingdom *come.* Thy will *be done.*
7. If it *bear* the test, it will be accepted.

8. If it *bears* the test, it will not be used.
9. *See* that thou *tell* no man.
10. Some heavenly power *guide* us hence.
11. *Judge* not, that ye *be* not *judged*.
12. *Beware*, lest thou *be led* into temptation.
13.   Last night the moon *had* a golden ring,
   And to-night no moon we *see*. — LONGFELLOW.
14. If fortune *serve* me, I'll requite this kindness. — SHAKESPEARE.

EXERCISE 93

(1) *Write three sentences, each containing verbs in the indicative mode.*

(2) *Write three sentences, each containing verbs in the subjunctive mode.*

(3) *Write three sentences, each containing verbs in the imperative mode.*

CHAPTER XLVII

THE INFINITIVE

(1) Select from the following sentences verb forms that do not assert, but that name actions, like nouns; (2) tell how they are used: —

1. To err is human.
2. They intend to return soon.
3. Doing nothing is tiresome.

The verb form that does not assert, but that merely names action or being, like a noun, is called an *infinitive*.

There are two infinitives, the *simple infinitive*, and the *infinitive* in *-ing*.

The simple infinitive is the simple form of the verb, alone or preceded by **to**; as, —

They can *go*.   I expect *to go*.

The simple form, without **to**, is used alone, or after a few of the most common verbs, such as *may, can, must, shall, will, bid, dare, do, let, make, need, hear,* and *see ;* as, Why not *sing ?   Do sing*.

The form with **to** is employed in most of the uses of the simple infinitive.[1]

The infinitive in -ing, also called the **participial infinitive** or **gerund**, is formed by adding *-ing* to the simple form of the verb; as, —

Learn the luxury of *doing* good.

The infinitive, like a noun, is used as subject or object; and, like a verb, it may take an object, if transitive, and may have adverbial modifiers; as, —

1. *To retreat* is impossible.
2. I decided *to remain* at home.
3. There is no prospect of *finding* the treasure.

---

[1] *To* was originally a preposition, used with the infinitive only in certain relations.   It is now a mere prefix, or sign of the infinitive in most of its uses.   As this is the only one of the infinitive forms that is distinctive, it is commonly called *the infinitive*.   The other forms are, however, equally true infinitives in origin and in use.

EXERCISE 94

Classify the infinitives in the following sentences, giving reasons for your statements :—

1. I like to look on a scene like this.

2. Let music swell the breeze.

3. The rain had ceased to patter, and now began to fall with a steady determination.

4. There was no difficulty in finding the river.

5. But where to find that happiest spot below,
   Who can direct, when all pretend to know?— GOLDSMITH.

6. A man has no more right to say an uncivil thing than to act one.— DR. JOHNSON.

7. He hears the parson pray and preach.— LONGFELLOW.

8. As he approached the stream, his heart began to thump.
   — IRVING.

9. But it must be understood that we did not go to see the Pyramids. We went only to look at them.— AMELIA B. EDWARDS.

10. There are two opposite ways by which some men make a figure in the world; one by talking faster than they think, and the other by holding their tongues and not thinking at all.— IRVING.

EXERCISE 95

Write sentences containing (1) *simple infinitives ;* (2) *participial infinitives formed from the following verbs :—*

find	break	choose	lose	sell
build	hear	spend	meet	have

CHAPTER XLVIII

THE PARTICIPLE

Tell of what verbs the italicized words are forms, and which parts of speech they most resemble: —

1. Out came the children *running*.
2. We beheld a horseman *approaching* leisurely.
3. The company, *seated* round the fire, welcomed the stranger.
4. We sailed by an island *covered* with large trees.

The verb form that is used as an adjective is called a *participle*. The participle does not assert, but assumes or implies action or being. It takes modifiers like a verb, but qualifies a noun or pronoun, like an adjective. The participle of a transitive verb takes an object.

A participle that denotes unfinished action is a *present* or *imperfect participle*; as, *hearing, writing.*

A participle that denotes finished action is a *past* or *perfect participle*; as, *heard, written.*

EXERCISE 96

Select the participles in the following sentences, state the kind, and tell what each modifies: —

1. I heard my own mountain goats bleating aloft. — CAMPBELL.

2.   Toiling, — rejoicing, — sorrowing,
         Onward through life he goes. — LONGFELLOW.

3. The passengers, warned by the helmsman, retreated into the cabin. — LOSSING.

4. While I lay musing on my pillow, I heard the sound of little feet pattering outside of the door. — IRVING.

5. Heaped in the hollows of the grove, the withered leaves lie dead. — BRYANT.

6. Looking out of the window, I saw a crow perched upon the edge of the nest. — BURROUGHS.

7. Yonder sat a tailor cross-legged, making a waistcoat; near him, stretched on his face at full length, sprawled a basket-maker with his half-woven basket and bundles of rushes beside him; and here, close against the main entrance, lay a blind man and his dog; the master asleep, the dog keeping watch. — AMELIA B. EDWARDS.

8. Truth, crushed to earth, shall rise again. — BRYANT.

EXERCISE 97

(1) *Copy from your Reader six sentences containing present participles. Underline the participles.*

(2) *Copy from your Reader six sentences containing perfect participles.*

FORMS OF THE VERB IN -*ing*

The verb form ending in -*ing* has four uses : —

(1) As a **present participle** ; thus, —

He hears his daughter's voice, *singing* in the village choir.

— LONGFELLOW.

(2) As an **infinitive** ; thus, —

They spent the evening in *singing* carols.

(3) As a **noun** ; thus, —

The time of the *singing* of birds has come. — BIBLE.

(4) As an **adjective** ; thus, —

A *singing* bird on every bough. — HOWITT.

It will be observed from the foregoing examples, that the present participle and the infinitive in *-ing* both have some of the constructions of the verb, but that the participle is an adjective in its use, while the infinitive is a noun. The verbal noun is similar to the infinitive, but it is more decidedly a noun, while the infinitive is more decidedly a verb. Thus the verbal noun may have an article and be joined to a following noun by a preposition, just as an ordinary noun may be, but it cannot take an object as an infinitive can.

EXERCISE 98

Distinguish between the different forms of the verb in **-ing** *in the following sentences, and tell how each is used:* —

1. The darting swallows soar and sing.
2. After standing a long time at the end of the wharf, gazing seaward, the strangers began to stray into the town.
3. Coming back we met two or three more regiments.
4. I had now given up all expectation of finding the road.
5. One could wander for miles through this forest without meeting a person, or hearing a sound, other than the occasional chatter of a squirrel, the song of a bird, or the sighing of the wind through the branches overhead.

6.   Hark! from the murmuring clods I hear
          Glad voices of the coming year.— BRYANT.

7. There's a merry brown thrush sitting up in a tree.

— LUCY LARCOM.

8.   But sorrow returned with the dawning of morn,
          And the voice in my dreaming ear melted away.

—CAMPBELL.

EXERCISE 99

Write three sentences, each containing a form of the verb in -ing used (1) *as a participial infinitive;* (2) *as a verbal noun;* (3) *as a present participle;* (4) *as a participial adjective.*

CHAPTER XLIX

TENSE

Tell what time each verb expresses in the following sentences, and mention the different forms of the verb:—

1. I see the light.
2. I saw the light.
3. I shall see the light.

The form of the verb that expresses the time of the action is called *tense.*

Since there are three divisions of time—present, past, and future, there are three leading tenses—present, past, and future.

A verb that denotes present time is in the *present tense;* as, I *hear.*

A verb that denotes past time is in the *past tense;* as, I *heard.*

A verb that denotes future time is in the *future tense;* as, I *shall hear.*

Besides these three leading tenses, there are three **perfect tenses**, which denote action as finished or completed.

A verb that denotes an action as completed at the *present* time is in the *present perfect tense;* as, —

> I *have heard* the speaker.
> He *has finished* the work.

A verb that denotes an action as having been completed before some *past* time is in the *past perfect* or *pluperfect tense;* as, —

> He *had heard* the report.

A verb that denotes an action which is to be completed before some future time is in the *future perfect tense;* as, —

> I *shall have heard* the lecture.
> He *will have heard* the lecture.

FORMATION OF TENSES

Tell which tenses are indicated by the form of the verb itself, and which are made by the aid of other verbs: —

TENSES OF THE INDICATIVE MODE

PRESENT.	I *write*	PRESENT PERFECT.	I *have written*
PAST.	I *wrote*	PAST PERFECT.	I *had written*
FUTURE.	I *shall write*	FUTURE PERFECT.	I *shall have written*

Only two tenses, the present and the past, are indicated by the form of the verb itself. The other tenses are expressed by the aid of other verbs, called **auxiliary** verbs.

The future tense is made up of the verb *shall* or *will* and the simple infinitive of the verb expressing the action.

Shall is used in the first person, and *will* in the second and third persons, to announce future action.　(See Chapter LIII.)

The present perfect tense is made up of the present of the auxiliary verb *have* and the perfect participle of the principal verb.

The past perfect tense is made up of the past of the auxiliary verb *have* and the perfect participle of the principal verb.

The future perfect tense is made up of the auxiliary *shall* or *will* and the perfect infinitive of the verb expressing the action.

EXERCISE 100

Point out the verbs in the following sentences, and name the tense of each : —

1. We started late in the afternoon of the first day.
2. There is a land of pure delight.
3. I had now come in sight of the house.
4. A ship-of-war arrived unexpectedly in the bay.
5. The walls of this most curious and interesting fortress have probably lost much of their original height.
6. Over the sea our galleys went.
7. The moon had risen, but the breeze had dropped.
8. A cuckoo's nest is a very simple affair, but it will bear close study. — M. THOMPSON.

9.　　　Short space he stood, — then waved his hand :
　　　　Down sunk the disappearing band. — SCOTT.

10. It is a strange thing how little, in general, people know about the sky. — RUSKIN.

11. Other soldiers heard the noise, and ran hastily from the barracks to assist their comrades. — HAWTHORNE.

12.　　　　My heart leaps up when I behold
　　　　　　A rainbow in the sky;
　　　　So was it when my life began,
　　　　So is it now I am a man. — WORDSWORTH.

EXERCISE 101

Write six tense forms for each of the following verbs, to be used with the subject I : —

find	break	come	drive	forget
give	know	see	draw	sell

CHAPTER L

PERSON AND NUMBER

Tell how many forms of the verb *hear* are used with the different subjects in the following, and give the endings of the special forms : —

	SINGULAR	PLURAL
First Person.	I hear	We hear
Second Person.	Thou hearest	You hear
Third Person.	He hears	They hear

The different forms that a verb takes to correspond to the person and the number of its subject are called *person* and *number* forms.

The second person singular has the ending *est* or *st* in

both the present and the past tenses of the indicative mode; as, —

> *Present.* Thou plant*est;*   thou see*st.*
> *Past.*   Thou planted*st;* thou saw*st.*

The third person singular has, in the present indicative, the ending *s* or *es* and the old forms *eth* or *th;* as, —

> She sleep*s* or she sleep*eth.*
> He do*es* or he do*th* or he do*eth.*

The forms with *thou* and the forms in *th* or *eth* are now seldom used, except in prayer and in poetry.

With the exception of the verb *be*, the first person singular and the plural forms for all the persons have no endings to mark person or number.

The verb *be* has different forms for the singular and the plural in the present and past tenses of the indicative mode; as, —

SINGULAR	PLURAL
I *am*	We, you, or they *are*
I *was*	We, you, or they *were*

EXERCISE 102

Write the forms of the following verbs required for the subjects **I, thou, he,** *and* **we,** *in the indicative present:* —

draw	hear	move	speak	sing
see	stand	choose	lift	come
find	forget	know	take	stand

CHAPTER LI

FORMS OF VERBS

Tell how the past tenses of the following verbs are formed: —

PRESENT	PAST	PERF. PART.	PRESENT	PAST	PERF. PART.
plant	planted	planted	fall	fell	fallen
look	looked	looked	throw	threw	thrown
live	lived	lived	give	gave	given

A verb that forms its past tense by adding *ed* or *d* to the present is a *regular verb;* as, *walk, walked; move, moved.*

A verb that does not form its past tense by adding *ed* or *d* to the present is an *irregular verb;* as, *drive, drove; give, gave.*

Some verbs have both regular and irregular forms; as, *build, builded* or *built; kneel, kneeled* or *knelt.*

Verbs that have more than one form for the past tense or perfect participle are said to be **redundant.**

The present tense, the past tense, and the perfect participle are called the *principal parts* of a verb, since all the other parts can be found when these three parts are known.

A verb that lacks any of the principal parts is called **defective;** as, —

PRESENT	PAST	PERFECT PARTICIPLE
can	could	————
may	might	————
shall	should	————
will	would	————

LIST OF IRREGULAR VERBS

PRESENT	PAST	PERF. PART.	PRESENT	PAST	PERF. PART.
abide	abode	abode	burn	burned / burnt	burned / burnt
arise	arose	arisen	burst	burst	burst
awake	awoke / awaked	awoke / awaked	buy	bought	bought
bear [to bring forth]	bore	born / borne	cast	cast	cast
			catch	caught	caught
bear [to carry]	bore	borne	chide	chid	chidden
beat	beat	beaten / beat	choose	chose	chosen
begin	began	begun	cleave [to split]	clove / cleft	cloven, *adj.* / cleft
behold	beheld	beheld	cling	clung	clung
bend	bent	bent	clothe	clothed / clad	clothed / clad
bereave	bereft	bereaved, *adj.* / bereft	come	came	come
			cost	cost	cost
beseech	besought	besought	creep	crept	crept
bid	bade / bid	bidden / bid	cut	cut	cut
bind	bound	bound	deal	dealt	dealt
			dig	dug	dug
bite	bit	bitten / bit	do	did	done
blow	blew	blown	draw	drew	drawn
break	broke	broken	dream	dreamed / dreamt	dreamed / dreamt
breed	bred	bred			
bring	brought	brought	drink	drank	drunken, *adj.* / drunk, drank
build	built	built	drive	drove	driven

Present	Past	Perf. Part.	Present	Past	Perf. Part.
dwell	dwelt	dwelt	hide	hid	hidden
eat	ate	eaten	hit	hit	hit
fall	fell	fallen	hold	held	held
feed	fed	fed	hurt	hurt	hurt
feel	felt	felt	keep	kept	kept
fight	fought	fought	kneel	{ kneeled	kneeled
find	found	found		knelt	knelt
flee	fled	fled	knit	{ knitted	knitted
fling	flung	flung		knit	knit
fly	flew	flown	know	knew	known
forbear	forbore	forborne	lay	laid	laid
forget	forgot	forgotten	lead	led	led
forsake	forsook	forsaken	lean	{ leaned	leaned
freeze	froze	frozen		leant	leant
get	got	{ gotten	leap	{ leaped	leaped
		got		leapt	leapt
gild	gilded	{ gilded	learn	{ learned	learned
		gilt, *adj.*		learnt	learnt
gird	{ girded	girded	leave	left	left
	girt	girt	lend	lent	lent
give	gave	given	let	let	let
go	went	gone	lie [to recline]	{ lay	lain
grind	ground	ground			
grow	grew	grown	light	{ lighted	lighted
hang	{ hung	hung		lit	lit
	hanged	hanged	lose	lost	lost
have	had	had	make	made	made
hear	heard	heard	mean	meant	meant
heave	{ hove	hove	meet	met	met
	heaved	heaved			

Present	Past	Perf. Part.	Present	Past	Perf. Part.
pass	passed	passed / past	shred	shred	shred
pay	paid	paid	shrink	shrank	shrunk
pen	penned / pent	penned / pent	shut	shut	shut
put	put	put	sing	sang	sung
quit	quitted / quit	quitted / quit	sink	sank	sunken, *adj.* / sunk
read	read	read	sit	sat	sat
rend	rent	rent	slay	slew	slain
ride	rode	ridden	sleep	slept	slept
ring	rang	rung	slide	slid	slidden / slid
rise	rose	risen	sling	slung	slung
run	ran	run	slink	slunk	slunk
say	said	said	slit	slit	slit
see	saw	seen	smell	smelled / smelt	smelled / smelt
seek	sought	sought	smite	smote	smitten
seethe	seethed	sodden, *adj.* / seethed	sow	sowed	sown / sowed
sell	sold	sold	speak	spoke	spoken
send	sent	sent	speed	sped	sped
set	set	set	spell	spelled / spelt	spelled / spelt
shake	shook	shaken	spend	spent	spent
shed	shed	shed	spill	spilt	spilt
shine	shone	shone	spin	spun	spun
shoe	shod	shod	spread	spread	spread
shoot	shot	shot	spring	sprang	sprung
show	showed	shown / showed			

Present	Past	Perf. Part.	Present	Past	Perf. Part.
stand	stood	stood	thrive	throve / thrived	thriven / thrived
steal	stole	stolen			
sting	stung	stung	throw	threw	thrown
strew	strewed	strewn / strewed	thrust	thrust	thrust
stride	strode	stridden	tread	trod	trodden / trod
strike	struck	stricken / struck	wake	woke / waked	woke / waked
string	strung	strung	wear	wore	worn
strive	strove	striven	weave	wove	woven
swear	swore	sworn	weep	wept	wept
sweat	sweat	sweat	wet	wetted / wet	wetted / wet
sweep	swept	swept			
swim	swam	swum	win	won	won
swing	swung	swung	wind	wound	wound
take	took	taken	work	worked	wrought, *adj.* / worked
teach	taught	taught			
tear	tore	torn	wring	wrung	wrung
tell	told	told	write	wrote	written
think	thought	thought			

CHAPTER LII

AUXILIARY VERBS

Compare the italicized verbs in the following sentences, and tell which express their own proper meanings and which help other verbs to express their meanings: —

1. Trees *have* roots.   2. The leaves *have* fallen.

3. It *was* an ancient mariner.

4. How cheerfully the week *was* spent!

Verbs that are used to help or complete the conjugation of other verbs, are said to be used as *auxiliaries,* and are then called *auxiliary* verbs; as,—

> The rain *had* ceased.

EXERCISE 103

Point out the verbs in the following sentences, and show which are used as auxiliary verbs : —

1. The days are cold, the nights are long.
2. The sower's task is done.
3. Some of the men had no muskets, and almost all were without bayonets.
4. The boats had difficulty in landing.
5. I have had playmates : I have had companions.
6. By fairy hands their knell is rung.
7. There was a sound of revelry by night.
8. The cabin was surrounded by a dense forest.
9. They know not what they do.
10. He did receive the message.
11. His face did shine as the sun.
12. I shall not look upon his like again.
13. If I will that he tarry till I come, what is that to thee?
14. He will not do the work.
15. Who trusts the strength will with the burden grow.
16.   The mountain and the squirrel
        Had a quarrel.

The verbs *have, do, shall, will,* and *be* are used as auxiliary verbs with the participles or infinitives of other verbs to form tense and voice. They have the following forms : —

I.—THE VERB *Have*

PRINCIPAL PARTS

PRESENT	PAST	PERFECT PARTICIPLE
Have	had	had

INDICATIVE MODE

PRESENT TENSE		PAST TENSE	
SINGULAR	PLURAL	SINGULAR	PLURAL
I have	We have	I had	We had
Thou[1] hast	You have	Thou hadst	You had
He has	They have	He had	They had

SUBJUNCTIVE MODE

PRESENT TENSE		PAST TENSE	
SINGULAR	PLURAL	SINGULAR	PLURAL
(If) I have	(If) we have	(If) I had	(If) we had
(If) thou have	(If) you have	(If) thou had	(If) you had
(If) he have	(If) they have	(If) he had	(If) they had

IMPERATIVE MODE

SINGULAR	PLURAL
Have (thou)	Have (ye *or* you)

INFINITIVES

(To) have	Having

PARTICIPLES

PRESENT	PERFECT
Having	had

[1] In ordinary speech, the pronoun *you* has taken the place of the singular form *thou;* but *you* is plural, and takes a plural verb.

Have as an Auxiliary Verb

The verb *have* is used as auxiliary with the perfect participle of a verb, to form the perfect tenses, each part of *have* forming the corresponding perfect; as, —

Present Perfect.	I have seen
Past Perfect.	I had seen
Future Perfect.	I shall have seen
Perfect Infinitives.	(To) have seen; having seen
Perfect Participle.	Having seen

Have as an Independent Verb

When *have* expresses possession it is an independent verb; as, —

Birds of the air *have* nests.

EXERCISE 104

Tell whether the verb have *in the following sentences is an independent verb or an auxiliary verb, giving a reason in each case:* —

1. If you have tears, prepare to shed them now. — SHAKESPEARE.

2.   " Have then thy wish ! "   He whistled shrill,
   And he was answered from the hill. — SCOTT.

3. Yes: he had lived to shame me from my sneer. — TAYLOR.

4. The sun had scarcely risen when the messenger arrived.

5.   Greatly begin ! though you have time
   But for a line, be that sublime. — LOWELL.

6. The things which I have seen, I now can see no more.

7. The fondness for rural life among the higher classes of the English, has had a great and salutary effect upon the national character.
   — IRVING.

CHAPTER LIII

AUXILIARY VERBS. — *Continued*

II. — *Shall*

PRESENT TENSE		PAST TENSE	
SINGULAR	PLURAL	SINGULAR	PLURAL
I shall	We shall	I should	We should
Thou shalt	You shall	Thou shouldst	You should
He shall	They shall	He should	They should

III. — *Will*

PRESENT TENSE		PAST TENSE	
SINGULAR	PLURAL	SINGULAR	PLURAL
I will	We will	I would	We would
Thou wilt	You will	Thou wouldst	You would
He will	They will	He would	They would

Shall and *will* are used with the infinitive of a verb, to form the future tense. *Shall* is an auxiliary of the future in the first person, and *will* in the second and third persons; as, —

> I *shall* pass the house this afternoon.
> You *will* be too late.
> He *will* bring the papers.

To make a promise or to express the determination of the speaker, *will* is used in the first person and *shall* in the second and third persons; as, —

> I *will* do the errand.
> I *will* have my bond.
> You *shall* not escape.
> He *shall* receive the reward.

Shall is used in asking questions in the first person; as, —

Shall I ring the bell? (The action is dependent on the will of the person addressed.)

Either *shall* or *will* is used, according to the answer expected, in asking questions in the second and third persons; as, —

Shall you sign the paper? (I *shall* sign the paper.)
Will you give me the address? (I *will* give you the address.)

Should and *would*, in corresponding cases, are used in the same manner as *shall* and *will;* thus, —

I *shall* return the book, or I *should* return the book.
You *will* find the tree, or you *would* find the tree.

EXERCISE 105

Explain each use of **shall** *and of* **will** *in the following sentences:* —

1. To-day the vessel shall be launched. — LONGFELLOW.
2. Take care of your spirit and conduct, and your reputation will take care of itself. — HAMILTON.
3. You will compel me then to read the will. — SHAKESPEARE.
4. Shall I descend? And will you give me leave? — SHAKESPEARE.
5. Hear me, for I will speak. — SHAKESPEARE.
6. Will you be patient? Will you stay awhile? — SHAKESPEARE.
7. If we fail, it can be no worse for us. But we shall not fail. The cause will raise up armies; the cause will create navies. — WEBSTER.
8. All that breathe will share thy destiny. — BRYANT.
9. Choose ye this day whom ye will serve.

EXERCISE 106

(1) *Copy the following sentences, filling the blanks with a form of* **shall** *or* **will**. (2) *State a reason for the use of each word inserted* : —

1. We —— go if it does not rain.
2. —— you have hot or cold tea?
3. The work —— probably be finished to-night.
4. Whither thou goest, I —— go; and where thou lodgest, I —— lodge.
5. I —— lift up mine eyes unto the hills.
6. —— I find you at home?
7. He said he —— not accept the explanation.
8. I —— be pleased to hear from you.

CHAPTER LIV

AUXILIARY VERBS. — *Continued*

IV. — CONJUGATION OF THE VERB *Be*

PRINCIPAL PARTS

PRESENT	PAST	PERFECT PARTICIPLE
Be, am	was	been [1]

INDICATIVE MODE

PRESENT TENSE

SINGULAR	PLURAL
I am	We are
Thou art	You are
He is	They are

---

[1] The forms of the verb *be* are derived from three different verbs, now represented by the forms *be, am,* and *was.*

PAST TENSE

I was	We were
Thou wast (wert)	You were
He was	They were

FUTURE TENSE

I shall be	We shall be
Thou wilt be	You will be
He will be	They will be

PRESENT PERFECT TENSE

SINGULAR	PLURAL
I have been	We have been
Thou hast been	You have been
He has been	They have been

PAST PERFECT TENSE

I had been	We had been
Thou hadst been	You had been
He had been	They had been

FUTURE PERFECT TENSE

I shall have been	We shall have been
Thou wilt have been	You will have been
He will have been	They will have been

SUBJUNCTIVE MODE

PRESENT TENSE

SINGULAR	PLURAL
(If) I be	(If) we be
(If) thou be	(If) you be
(If) he be	(If) they be

PAST TENSE

(If) I were	(If) we were
(If) thou wert	(If) you were
(If) he were	(If) they were

IMPERATIVE MODE
PRESENT TENSE

SINGULAR	PLURAL
Be (thou)	Be (ye *or* you)

INFINITIVES

PRESENT (To) be	Being
PERFECT (To) have been	Having been

PARTICIPLES

PRESENT	PERFECT	COMPOUND PERFECT
Being	been	having been

Be as an Auxiliary Verb

The different forms of the verb *be* are used as auxiliary —

(1) With the perfect participle of a transitive verb to make the **passive voice**; as, —

I *am seen*	I *have been seen*
I *was seen*	I *had been seen*
I *shall be seen*	I *shall have been seen*

(2) With the present participle of a verb, to make the **progressive form.** The progressive form represents an action as continuing or progressing; as, —

I *am reading*	I *have been reading*
I *was reading*	I *had been reading*
I *shall be reading*	I *shall have been reading*

Be as an Independent Verb

When not thus used with the participle of another verb, *be* **is an independent verb.** It may then —

(1) Express **existence**; as, God *is*.

(2) Be used as a **copula,** connecting its subject to a word or words describing the subject; as, Life *is* real.

EXERCISE 107

Explain the use of the verb **be** *in each of the following examples :* —

1. Life is real! Life is earnest! — LONGFELLOW.

2. I have been a stranger in a strange land.

3. The harp, his sole remaining joy,
    Was carried by an orphan boy. — SCOTT.

4. Yarmouth was a walled town, and a good part of the ancient enclosure has been preserved.

5. If money had been needed before, it was still more needed now.

6. This was accomplished in less than an hour's time.

7. Trade with the colonies was forbidden.

8.   Old Kaspar's work was done,
    And he before his cottage door
       Was sitting in the sun. — SOUTHEY.

9. While we were talking, a third messenger arrived.

10. Somewhere the birds are singing evermore.

11. O sweet and strange it seems to me, that ere this day is done,
    The voice, that now is speaking, may be beyond the sun.
    — TENNYSON.

12. The city was destroyed by an earthquake.

13. The great iron gateway that opened into the courtyard was locked. — IRVING.

14. Whatever is, is right. — POPE.

15. The old stage-coach is at the door.

16.   I stood on the bridge at midnight,
         As the clocks were striking the hour.

EXERCISE 108

Copy from the sentences in this lesson (1) *all verbs that have the passive form;* (2) *all verbs that have the progressive form; and explain the formation and the use of each.*

EXERCISE 109

(1) *Write five sentences, each containing the verb* **be** *used as an independent verb.*

(2) *Write five sentences, each containing a verb in the passive voice.*

(3) *Write five sentences, each containing a verb in the progressive form.*

V. — THE VERB *Do*

Do as an Auxiliary Verb

The present and past tenses of the verb *do* are used as auxiliaries with the simple infinitive —

(1) In **emphatic** assertions; as, —

    I *do wish* you would listen. I *did listen.*

(2) In **interrogative** sentences; as, —

    Do you *hear* the bell? *Did* you *see* the sail?

(3) In **negative** sentences; as, —

    I *do* not *hear* the bell. I *did* not *see* a sail.

Do as an Independent Verb

When *do* is used with the meaning *to perform,* it is an independent verb; as, *Do* your duty. He *did* the work quickly.

EXERCISE 110

Tell whether the verb **do** *is used as an independent or as an auxiliary verb in the following examples, and explain the use of the auxiliaries : —*

1. The evil that men do lives after them. — SHAKESPEARE.
2. You all did mark how he did shake. — SHAKESPEARE.
3. She gave me of the tree, and I did eat.
4. You all do know this mantle. — SHAKESPEARE.
5. I do not like your faults.
6.   Accuse not nature ; she hath done her part :
       Do thou but thine. — MILTON.
7. Do not dissipate your energies on trifles. — HAMILTON.
8. Most of the facts of nature, especially in the life of birds and animals, are well screened. We do not see the play, because we do not look intently enough. — JOHN BURROUGHS.
9. Did ye not hear it? — BYRON.
10. A merry heart doeth good like a medicine.

CHAPTER LV

AUXILIARY VERBS — *Continued*

The following verbs are used with the simple infinitive to express power, permission, possibility, necessity, etc. They are sometimes called **auxiliaries of mode.**

I. — *Can*

PRESENT TENSE		PAST TENSE	
SINGULAR	PLURAL	SINGULAR	PLURAL
I can	We can	I could	We could
Thou canst	You can	Thou couldst	You could
He can	They can	He could	They could

Can is used to express power or ability, and is in the indicative mode; as, —

> She *can* walk.
>
> He *could* speak readily in three or four languages.

II. — *May*

PRESENT TENSE		PAST TENSE	
SINGULAR	PLURAL	SINGULAR	PLURAL
I may	We may	I might	We might
Thou mayest	You may	Thou mightest	You might
He may	They may	He might	They might

May expresses permission or possibility; as, —

> You *may* [*are permitted* to] enter the room.
>
> He *may* [it *is possible* that he will] change his mind.

May is also used to express purpose, or to express a wish; as, —

> Open the gate that they *may* enter.
>
> *May* you be happy.

Could and *might* are sometimes used as the simple past of *can* and *may*, and sometimes in a conditional sense; as, —

> I *could* hear the music.
>
> The lights of the village *might* be seen from the bay.
>
> He *might* go if he *could* spare the time.

III. — *Must*

Must has no change of form. It expresses necessity; as —

He *must* have rest.

IV. — *Should* and *Would* [1]

Should is no longer used as a simple past, but has the sense of an indefinite present or of a contingent condition; as, —

Ambition *should* be made of sterner stuff.

If I *should* begin the work, I could not finish it.

---

[1] The phrases made up of the verbs *may, can, must, might, could, would,* or *should,* with an infinitive, are classed together by some grammarians, and called the **potential mode**. A verb in the so-called potential mode is conjugated as follows: —

PRESENT TENSE

SINGULAR	PLURAL
I may go	We may go
Thou mayst go	You may go
He may go	They may go

PAST TENSE

I might go	We might go
Thou mightst go	You might go
He might go	They might go

PRESENT PERFECT TENSE

I may have gone	We may have gone
Thou mayst have gone	You may have gone
He may have gone	They may have gone

PAST PERFECT TENSE

I might have gone	We might have gone
Thou mightst have gone	You might have gone
He might have gone	They might have gone

Would is sometimes a simple past, sometimes a contingent present; as, —

> He *would* not speak when he had the opportunity.
> He *would* not speak if he had the opportunity.

V. — *Ought*

Ought is the old past tense of the verb *owe*, and expresses duty or obligation. It is used with the present infinitive to indicate present time, and with the perfect infinitive to indicate past time; as, —

> *Present.* He ought to go.
> *Past.* He ought to have gone.

EXERCISE 111

Tell how the verbs **may, can, must, should,** *and* **would** *are used in the following sentences :* —

1. Lives of great men all remind us
   We can make our lives sublime. — LONGFELLOW.

2. For men may come and men may go,
   But I go on forever. — TENNYSON.

3. He that fights and runs away,
   May live to fight another day.

4. It may be the gulfs will wash us down ;
   It may be we shall touch the Happy Isles.

5. Wealth may seek us, but wisdom must be sought.

6. It is not what a lawyer tells me I may do, but what humanity, reason, and justice tell me I ought to do. — BURKE.

7.   They had been friends in youth,
          But whispering tongues can poison truth.

8. Too late! too late! ye cannot enter now. — TENNYSON.

9. How he could trot! how he could run! and then such leaps
as he could take — there was not a hedge in the whole country that
he could not clear. — IRVING.

10. She must weep or she will die. — TENNYSON.

11. He saw that it would be dark long before he could reach the
village. — IRVING.

12.   If a storm should come and awake the deep,
          What matter! I shall ride and sleep. — PROCTER.

EXERCISE 112

Write sentences illustrating the correct use of the verbs
may, can, must, might, could, should, *and* ***would.***

CHAPTER LVI

CONJUGATION OF THE VERB *Drive*

PRINCIPAL PARTS

PRESENT	PAST	PERFECT PARTICIPLE
Drive	drove	driven

I. — ACTIVE VOICE

INDICATIVE MODE

PRESENT TENSE

SINGULAR	PLURAL
I drive	We drive
Thou drivest	You drive
He drives	They drive

PAST TENSE

I drove	We drove
Thou drovest	You drove
He drove	They drove

FUTURE TENSE

I shall drive	We shall drive
Thou wilt drive	You will drive
He will drive	They will drive

PRESENT PERFECT TENSE

I have driven	We have driven
Thou hast driven	You have driven
He has driven	They have driven

PAST PERFECT TENSE

Singular	Plural
I had driven	We had driven
Thou hadst driven	You had driven
He had driven	They had driven

FUTURE PERFECT TENSE

I shall have driven	We shall have driven
Thou wilt have driven	You will have driven
He will have driven	They will have driven

SUBJUNCTIVE MODE

PRESENT TENSE

Singular	Plural
(If) I drive	(If) we drive
(If) thou drive	(If) you drive
(If) he drive	(If) they drive

PAST TENSE

(If) I drove   (If) we drove
(If) thou drove   (If) you drove
(If) he drove   (If) they drove

IMPERATIVE MODE

PRESENT TENSE

SINGULAR   PLURAL

Drive (thou)   Drive (ye *or* you)

INFINITIVES

PRESENT (To) drive   Driving
PERFECT (To) have driven   Having driven

PARTICIPLES

PRESENT   **PERFECT**   **COMPOUND PERFECT**

Driving   ————   having driven

II. — PASSIVE FORMS

The *passive forms* of a transitive verb are made by joining its perfect participle to the different forms of the verb *be;* thus, —

INDICATIVE MODE

PRESENT TENSE

I am driven

PRESENT PERFECT TENSE

I have been driven

PAST TENSE

I was driven

PAST PERFECT TENSE

I had been driven

FUTURE TENSE

I shall be driven

FUTURE PERFECT TENSE

I shall have been driven

SUBJUNCTIVE MODE

PRESENT TENSE

(If) I be driven

PAST TENSE

(If) I were driven

IMPERATIVE MODE

PRESENT TENSE

Be (thou) driven

INFINITIVES

PRESENT (To) be driven
PERFECT (To) have been driven

Being driven
Having been driven

PARTICIPLES

PRESENT	**PERFECT**	**COMPOUND PERFECT**
Being driven	driven	having been driven

III — PROGRESSIVE FORMS

The *progressive forms* of a verb are made by joining its present participle to the different forms of the verb *be;* thus, —

INDICATIVE MODE

PRESENT TENSE

I am driving

PRESENT PERFECT TENSE

I have been driving

PAST TENSE

I was driving

PAST PERFECT TENSE

I had been driving

FUTURE TENSE

I shall be driving

FUTURE PERFECT TENSE

I shall have been driving

SUBJUNCTIVE MODE

PRESENT TENSE

(If) I be driving

PAST TENSE

(If) I were driving

IMPERATIVE MODE

PRESENT TENSE

Be (thou driving)

INFINITIVES

PRESENT (To) be driving

PERFECT (To) have been driving

Having been driving

PARTICIPLES

PRESENT	**PERFECT**	**COMPOUND PERFECT**
————	————	having been driving

EXERCISE 113

Write the active forms of the verb **see** *that are used with the subject* **I** *in the different modes and tenses.*

EXERCISE 114

Write the passive forms of the verb **see** *that are used with the subject* **thou** *in the different modes and tenses.*

EXERCISE 115

Write the progressive forms of the verb **write** *that are used with the subject* **he** *in the different modes and tenses.*

CHAPTER LVII

DIRECTIONS FOR PARSING VERBS, INFINITIVES, AND PARTICIPLES

I. VERBS

To parse a verb, tell —

1. Its **conjugation** — regular or irregular, giving its principal parts.
2. Its **class** — transitive or intransitive.
3. Its **voice** — active or passive (if transitive).
4. Its **mode** — indicative, subjunctive, or imperative.
5. Its **tense.**
6. Its **person** and **number.**
7. Its **subject.**

EXAMPLE 1. — A flat stone *marks* the spot where the bard *is buried.*

Marks is a regular verb — mark, marked, marked. It is transitive, active voice, indicative mode, present tense, third person, singular number, agreeing with its subject *stone.*

Is buried is the passive form of the regular verb *bury,* — bury, buried, buried. It is transitive, passive voice, indicative mode, present tense, third person, singular number, agreeing with its subject *bard.*

EXAMPLE 2. — The dew *was falling* fast.

Was falling is the progressive form of the irregular verb *fall* — fall, fell, fallen. It is intransitive, indicative mode, past tense, third person, singular number, agreeing with its subject *dew.*

EXAMPLE 3. — I may do that I *shall be* sorry for.

Shall be, made up of the auxiliary *shall* and the simple infinitive of the verb *be*, is the future tense of the verb *be*. It is irregular, — be, was, been, — intransitive, indicative mode, used with the subject *I*.

EXAMPLE 4. — *Be* silent, that you may hear.

Be is an irregular verb — be, was, been — intransitive, imperative mode, present tense, used with the subject *you* understood.

EXERCISE 116

Parse the verbs in the following sentences: —

1. Have patience with me, and I will pay thee all.
2. Now stir the fire, and close the shutters fast. — COWPER.
3. The ship is sinking beneath the tide. — SOUTHEY.
4. I have been young, and now am old, yet have I not seen the righteous forsaken. — BIBLE.

5.   There is a tide in the affairs of men,
      Which, taken at the flood, leads on to fortune;
      Omitted, all the voyage of their life
      Is bound in shallows and in miseries. — SHAKESPEARE.

6. The broad sun above laughed a pitiless laugh.
7. The Americans were sheltered by an intervening wood.

8.   Some murmur when their sky is clear
      And wholly bright to view,
    If one small speck of dark appear
      In their great heaven of blue. — TRENCH.

9. I dreamed to-night that I did feast with Cæsar.
10. We had had no water since our daylight breakfast; our lunch on the mountain had been moistened only by the fog.

           — C. D. WARNER.

Auxiliaries of Mode

In phrases made up of *can* (*could*), *may* (*might*), *must*, *should*, or *would*, with the simple infinitive, parse the auxiliary verb and the infinitive separately.[1]

Example 1. — How he *could run!*

Could is a defective verb, transitive, indicative mode, past tense, used with the subject *he*. *Run* is the present infinitive of the verb *run*. It is intransitive, object of the verb *could*.

Example 2. — If you were here, I *could assist* you.

Could is a defective verb, transitive, subjunctive mode, past tense, used with the subject *I*. *Assist* is the present infinitive of the verb *assist*. It is transitive, active voice, object of the verb *could*.

Example 3. — He *should have gone.*

Should is a defective verb, transitive, indicative mode, past tense, used with the subject *he*. *Have gone* is the perfect infinitive of the verb *go*. It is intransitive, object of the verb *should*.

EXERCISE 117

Parse the italicized verbs in the following sentences: —

1. Have patience, gentle friends, I *must* not *read* it.
2. One *may acquire* the habit of looking upon the sunny side of things, and he *may* also *acquire* the habit of looking upon the gloomy side.

---

[1] These compound forms are sometimes parsed as verb-phrases in the indicative or subjunctive mode, according to their use in the sentence.

3. *Should* he *go*, he *could* not *hear* the lecture.

4. We *should be* as careful of our words as of our actions.

5. He *could speak* readily in three or four languages.

6. Give me this water that I *may* not *thirst*.

7. If you *would achieve* a high success, you *must think* for yourself.

8. If I were you, I *should attempt* the work.

9. The guards told us that we *could proceed* no farther.

II. INFINITIVES

To parse an infinitive, tell —

1. From what **verb** it is derived.

2. Its **form** — present or perfect, active or passive.

3. Its **syntax** — use in the sentence.

EXAMPLE 1. — The greatest curiosity of the study remains *to be mentioned*.

To be mentioned is a simple infinitive from the transitive verb *mention*. It is present, passive, and depends upon the verb *remains*.

EXAMPLE 2. — Form the habit of *listening* attentively.

Listening is an infinitive from the verb *listen*. It is present active, and is used as the object of the preposition *of*.

EXERCISE 118

Parse the infinitives in the following sentences: —

1. To relieve the wretched was his pride.

2. Remember that when the inheritance devolves upon you, you are not only to enjoy, but to improve.

3. He had the happy knack of starting interesting subjects and saying all sorts of interesting things by the way.

4. Do with all your might whatever you have to do, without thinking of the future.

5. To see is to believe.

6. Seeing is believing.

7. In keeping Thy commandments there is great reward.

8. But talking is not always to converse.

III. PARTICIPLES

To parse a participle, tell —

1. From what **verb** it is derived.
2. Its **form** — present or perfect, active or passive.
3. Its **syntax** — use in the sentence.

EXAMPLE 1. — *Looking* upward, he saw the moon.

Looking is a present participle, active, from the verb *look*. It modifies the pronoun *he*.

EXAMPLE 2. — The ships, *anchored* in the harbor, were loaded with tea.

Anchored is a perfect participle, passive, from the verb *anchor*. It modifies the noun *ships*.

EXERCISE 119

Parse the verbs, the infinitives, and the participles in the following sentences : —

1. I rose softly, opened the door suddenly, and beheld one of the most beautiful little fairy groups that a painter could imagine. — IRVING.

2. Let us enter and pass up the staircase. — HAWTHORNE.

3. In this way they expected to ruin all the merchants, and starve the poor people, by depriving them of employment. — HAWTHORNE.

4. Let me move slowly through the street. — BRYANT.

5. The country was to be defended, and to be saved, before it could be enjoyed. — WEBSTER.

6. We cannot look, however imperfectly, upon a great man without gaining something by him. — CARLYLE.

7.   In an attitude imploring,
         Hands upon his bosom crossed,
      Wondering, worshipping, adoring,
         Knelt the Monk in rapture lost. — LONGFELLOW.

8. The rattle of drums, beaten out of all manner of time, was heard above every other sound. — HAWTHORNE.

9. Whatever may be our fate, be assured that this declaration will stand. It may cost treasure, and it may cost blood; but it will stand, and it will richly compensate for both.

10. You may break, you may shatter the vase, if you will,
      But the scent of the roses will hang round it still.

11. For men must work, and women must weep,
      Though storms be sudden, and waters deep.

12. The burden laid upon me
      Seemed greater than I could bear.

13. Modern majesty consists in work. What a man can do is his greatest ornament, and he always consults his dignity by doing it. — CARLYLE.

14. The pine, placed nearly always among scenes disordered and desolate, brings into them all possible elements of order and precision. Lowland trees may lean to this side and that, though it is but a meadow breeze that bends them, or a bank of cowslips from which their trunks lean aslope. But let storm and avalanche do their worst, and let the pine find only a ledge of vertical precipice to cling to, it will nevertheless grow straight. — RUSKIN.

CHAPTER LVIII

CORRECT USE OF VERBS

I. *Lay, Lie*

PRESENT	PAST	PRES. PARTICIPLE	PERF. PARTICIPLE
Lay	laid	laying	laid
Lie	lay	lying	lain

Lay is a transitive verb. It means to place or put something in position. *Lie* is an intransitive verb, meaning to rest.

EXERCISE 120

Copy the following sentences, filling the blanks with the proper form of lay or lie: —

1. —— the music on the piano.
2. The rain has —— the dust.
3. He —— down to rest.
4. He has —— there an hour.
5. She —— the letter on the desk.

6. The dog is —— by the fire.
7. The workmen are —— a new walk.
8. —— the roots with care.

9.   The gentle race of flowers
   Are —— in their lowly beds, with the fair and good of ours.

10. In the cold moist earth we —— her, when the forests cast
    the leaf.

II. *Sit, Set*

PRESENT	PAST	PRES. PARTICIPLE	PERF. PARTICIPLE
Sit	sat	sitting	sat
Set	set	setting	set

Sit is an intransitive verb. It means to take a seat; to remain in a seated or settled position; to perch or brood, as a bird.

Set is transitive when it means to place something in position; to fix or establish; it is intransitive when it means to sink or settle downward.

EXERCISE 121

Re-write the following sentences, using the proper verb or form from each parenthesis. Give a reason for your choice: —

1. I (set, sat) in this seat last night.
2. The hen is (sitting, setting) on twelve eggs.
3. He had (sat, set) under that tree for an hour.
4. The gardener is (sitting, setting) out strawberry plants.
5. Will you (set, sit) by me?

6. (Sit, set) the cup on the shelf.

7. The surgeon (set, sat) the boy's arm.

8. The sun is (setting, sitting) already.

9. Five little birds were (sitting, setting) in a row.

10. Who (sat, set) the table?

11. He (sat, set) in the front seat.

12. They were (setting, sitting) by the pond, watching the goldfish.

III. *May, Can*

May is used to indicate *permission* or *possibility*; *can*, to denote *power* or *ability*.

EXERCISE 122

Copy the following sentences, filling the blanks with the proper form of **may** *or* **can:** —

1. Mabel —— not sing.

2. He —— speak French fluently.

3. We —— not hear the speaker.

4. Who —— understand his errors?

5. You —— look at my drawings.

6. The boy said that he —— sail a boat.

7. —— you hear the watch tick?

8. —— you tell the names of our most common birds?

9. —— I go home?

10. I told him that he —— go.

IV. *Think, Guess, Expect*

To think is to judge, to exercise the mind. *To guess* is to form an opinion at random. *To expect* is to look forward to; this verb always refers to the future.

Copy the following sentences, filling the blanks with some form of think, guess, or expect: —

1. I will —— about the matter.
2. No one was able to —— the riddle.
3. Do you —— to meet your friend.
4. I —— he did not go.
5. I —— your plan is a wise one.
6. Do you —— the attendance will be large?
7. —— what I have in this box.
8. England —— every man to do his duty.

V. *Stop, Stay*

Stop, to cease from motion; to come to an end. *Stay*, to remain; to tarry.

EXERCISE 124

Copy the following sentences, filling the blanks with the proper form of **stop** *or* **stay**. *Give in each case a reason for your choice:* —

1. Did you —— at Chicago on your way home?
2. Where did you —— while you were in the city?
3. The driver is —— the car.
4. Mr. Hunt is —— at the Mountain House.
5. Does this boat —— at the first landing?
6. Our friends are —— at the seashore.
7. The plumber could not —— the leak.
8. You promised to —— at home this evening.
9. We shall —— here overnight.
10. Let us —— here, and wait for a car.

VI. *Learn, Teach*

Learn, to acquire knowledge; to receive instruction.
Teach, to give instruction to.

EXERCISE 125

*Copy the following sentences, filling the blanks with the proper form of **learn** or **teach**:* —

1. He —— the child to sing.
2. Clara —— her lesson quickly.
3. The pupils are —— a new song.
4. Where did this boy —— to speak French?
5. Who —— you to skate?
6. We are —— to sketch from nature.
7. Take my yoke upon you, and —— of me.
8.   There, in his noisy mansion skilled to rule,
        The village master —— his little school.
9. The teacher —— us a new song.
10. The master —— John, and John —— his lesson quickly.

CHAPTER LIX

REVIEW OF VERBS

EXERCISE 126

Define a verb. What is a transitive verb? What is an intransitive verb? Mention a word that may be a transitive verb in one sentence, and an intransitive verb in another.

What inflections have verbs? What is meant by *voice?* How many voices are there? What does each denote? How is the passive voice formed?

What is meant by mode? How many modes are there? Define, and give examples of each.

What is tense? Name the three leading tenses. Which tenses are indicated by inflection, and which by the aid of other verbs?

What person-forms has the verb? What number-forms?

How do the infinitive and the participle differ from the verb? How do they differ from each other? Which part of speech is the infinitive most like? The participle? Mention four different verbal forms ending in *-ing*, and state the characteristics of each.

What are the principal parts of a verb? What is a regular verb? An irregular verb? Name a verb that has both regular and irregular forms. Name a verb that has the same form for the present tense, the past tense, and the perfect participle.

What is meant by conjugating a verb?

When is a verb said to be used as an auxiliary? Mention three verbs that may be used as either independent or auxiliary verbs, and give examples of each use. What auxiliary is used in forming the passive voice? Which of the auxiliaries are tense auxiliaries? How are they used?

CHAPTER LX

CLASSES OF ADVERBS

I. CLASSIFICATION ACCORDING TO MEANING

Point out the adverbs in the following sentences, and tell what each expresses: —

1. Now came still evening on.
2. Ah! then and there was hurrying to and fro.
3. Days brightly came and calmly went.
4. It is a very difficult task.

(1) Adverbs that show *when* or *how often* are adverbs of *time;* as, *now, then, to-day, yesterday, early, presently, soon, always, often, once, twice, daily, again.*

(2) Adverbs that show *where* are adverbs of *place;* as, *here, there, hither, thither, hence, thence, somewhere, yonder, above, below, up, down, away, off, far.*

The word *there* is not always an adverb of place. Sometimes it is used merely to introduce a sentence, in order that the verb may be placed before its subject. When it is used to introduce a sentence in this manner, it is called an **expletive;** as, —

There [expletive] was a sound of revelry by night.
There [adverb of place] groups of merry children played.

(3) Adverbs that show *how* are adverbs of *manner;* as, *well, ill, badly, slowly, quickly, clearly, together, so, thus.*

(4) Adverbs that show *how much* are adverbs of *degree;* as, *very, much, little, only, almost, enough, quite, too, so, as.*

(5) **Adverbs that express *certainty* or *uncertainty* are *modal adverbs*;** as, *indeed, verily, possibly, perhaps.*

The words *yes* and *no* are sometimes called adverbs, but they are really equivalent to sentences; as, Will you go? *Yes* (= I will go).

Combinations of words used as single adverbs may be called **adverbial phrases;** as, *again and again, at last, at length, by and by, by far, in and out, in vain, now and then, out and out, through and through, up and down.*

EXERCISE 127

Point out the adverbs and the adverbial phrases in the following sentences, tell to which class each belongs, and what it modifies : —

1. A thousand hearts beat happily. — BYRON.
2. Down sunk the bell with a gurgling sound. — SOUTHEY.
3.   Then did the little maid reply,
     "Seven boys and girls are we." — WORDSWORTH.
4. Defect in manners is usually the defect of fine perceptions.
                                — EMERSON.
5.   On right, on left, above, below,
    Sprung up at once the lurking foe. — SCOTT.
6.   Swiftly, swiftly flew the ship,
    Yet she sailed softly too. — COLERIDGE.
7. The world is too much with us. — WORDSWORTH.
8.   How often, oh, how often
     I had wished that the ebbing tide
    Would bear me away on its bosom
      O'er the ocean wild and wide. — LONGFELLOW.

II. CLASSIFICATION ACCORDING TO USE

Tell how each adverb is used in the following sentences: —

1. The guests withdrew silently.
2. The tree lies where it fell.
3. Where can rest be found?

(1) **An adverb that simply modifies another word is a** *simple adverb;* as, He walked *rapidly.*

(2) **An adverb that not only modifies a word, but also connects the clause of which it is a part with the remainder of the sentence, is a** *conjunctive adverb;* as, He came *when* he was called.

The most common words of this class are *when, where, whence, whither, how,* and *why.* These are also called **adverbial conjunctions.**

(3) **An adverb that is used to ask a question is an** *interrogative adverb;* as, *Where* did he stand?

EXERCISE 128

Find the conjunctive and the interrogative adverbs in the following sentences, and tell how each is used: —

1. Why are we here?
2. Some murmur when their sky is clear.

3. You take my house when you do take the prop
   That doth sustain my house; you take my life
   When you do take the means whereby I live.
   — SHAKESPEARE.

4. When I look upon the tombs of the great, every emotion of envy dies in me.

5. Where are the flowers, the fair young flowers, that lately
sprang and stood
In brighter light, and softer airs, a beauteous sisterhood?

—BRYANT.

CHAPTER LXI

COMPARISON OF ADVERBS

Some adverbs, like adjectives, admit of comparison. A few are compared by inflection; as, *soon, sooner, soonest.* Most adverbs form the comparative and superlative degrees by the use of *more* and *most;* as, *wisely, more wisely, most wisely.*

The following adverbs are compared irregularly:—

POSITIVE	COMPARATIVE	SUPERLATIVE
badly, ill	worse	worst
far	farther, further	farthest, furthest
late	later	latest, last
little	less	least
much	more	most
nigh, near	nearer	nearest, next
well	better	best

EXERCISE 129

Write the comparison of the following adverbs:—

| last | often | swiftly | next | ill |
| nigh | more | well | fast | distinctly |

CHAPTER LXII

HOW TO PARSE ADVERBS

To parse an adverb, tell —

1. The **kind** of adverb.
2. Its **degree,** if comparative or superlative.
3. Its **construction** — what it modifies.

EXAMPLE 1. — He *then* touched *briefly* upon the prominent events of the Revolution.

Then is an adverb of time, modifying the verb *touched.*
Briefly is an adverb of manner, modifying the verb *touched.*

EXAMPLE 2. — I remember, I remember
The house *where* I was born.

Where is a conjunctive adverb, showing place. It modifies the verb *was born,* and connects the clause "where I was born" with the word *house.*

EXAMPLE 3. — *When* did he go?

When is an interrogative adverb of time, modifying the verb *did go.*

EXERCISE 130

Parse the adverbs and the adjectives in the following sentences : —

1. He lives long that lives well.
2. Still waters run deep.
3. Welcome her, all things youthful and sweet !

4. Then they praised him soft and low.

5. He drank of the water so cool and clear. — SOUTHEY.

6. How fast the flitting figures come ! — BRYANT.

7. Down swept the chill wind from the mountain peak.

8. The door in the mountain-side shut fast.

9. A wondrous portal opened wide. — BROWNING.

10. The tumult grew louder.

11. Louder still the minstrels blew.

12.   Colder and louder blew the wind,
            A gale from the Northeast. — LONGFELLOW.

13.   There in the twilight cold and gray,
            Lifeless, but beautiful, he lay. — LONGFELLOW.

14. And there lay the steed with his nostril all wide,
      But through it there rolled not the breath of his pride.

15. There is nothing like a primeval wood for color on a sunny day. — C. D. WARNER.

16. Why stand ye here all the day idle? — BIBLE.

17.   Oh ! what a tangled web we weave,
            When first we practice to deceive. — SCOTT.

18.   O Solitude ! where are the charms
            That sages have seen in thy face? — COWPER.

19. O, why should the spirit of mortal be proud? — KNOX.

20. The rain is falling where they lie. — BRYANT.

CHAPTER LXIII

ADVERBS DISTINGUISHED FROM ADJECTIVES

Tell whether the italicized words in the following sentences are adjectives or adverbs, giving a reason in each case : —

1. She looks *cold*.
2. She looked *coldly* on the project.
3. The apple feels *hard*.
4. He works *hard*.

Be careful to discriminate between an adjective used to complete the predicate and an adverb used to modify the verb. An adjective is used when the quality or condition of the subject is given, and an adverb, when the manner of the action is described; as, —

The child seems *happy* (adjective).
He lived *happily* (adverb).

Do not use an adjective where an adverb is required; as, —

I am *very* tired (not *real* tired).
He is *somewhat* better (not *some* better).
She answered *promptly* (not *prompt*).

In poetry an adjective is sometimes used for an adverb; as, —

Silent rows the gondolier.

Some adverbs are identical in form with adjectives; as, *much, little, far, ill, hard, loud, soft, fast.*

EXERCISE 131

Copy the following sentences, inserting the proper word from each parenthesis. Give in each case a reason for your choice : —

1. She looked (beautiful, beautifully).
2. How (charming, charmingly) she sang.
3. The sentinel stood (firm, firmly) at his post.
4. Set the tree (firm, firmly).
5. The judge looked (sharp, sharply) at the prisoner.
6. We climbed the hill (easy, easily).
7. This is an (uncommon, uncommonly) large tree.
8. The patient is (some, somewhat) better.
9. It was a (remarkable, remarkably) clear night.
10. He was an (unusual, unusually) interesting speaker.
11. I am (real, very) sorry that you cannot join our party.
12. This milk tastes (sour, sourly).
13. The boy reads (clear, clearly) and (distinct, distinctly).
14. He is (some, somewhat) hoarse.
15. The bell sounded (clear, clearly).
16. The notes of the grackle sound (harsh, harshly).
17. How (quiet, quietly) the snow falls !
18. The speaker did not quote that passage (accurate, accurately).

EXERCISE 132

REVIEW OF ADVERBS

What is an adverb? How are adverbs classified with respect to meaning? Give an example of each class. How are they classified with respect to use? State the two offices of a conjunctive adverb. Give an example of an interrogative adverb. Mention five adverbs that admit of comparison, and give the comparison of each. In what way are adjectives and adverbs alike? How do they differ?

CHAPTER LXIV

CLASSES OF PHRASES

I. CLASSIFICATION ACCORDING TO FORM

Read the phrases[1] in the following examples, and tell by what each phrase is introduced: —

1. The tree *on the corner* is an elm.
2. They walked *toward the river*.
3. He expects *to return soon*.
4. We found the boy *sailing a boat*.

(1) **A phrase introduced by a preposition is a *prepositional phrase;*** as, —

1. The leaves *of this plant* are glossy.
2. We heard the sound *of distant footsteps*.
3. The troops were marching *through a valley*.
4. He reads *for information*.

(2) **A phrase introduced by an infinitive is an *infinitive phrase;*** as, —

1. *To do good* should be the aim of all.
2. He hoped *to win the prize*.
3. Crowds came *to behold the sight*.

[1] See page 27.

(3) **A phrase introduced by a participle is a *participial phrase*;** as, —

1. *Looking upward,* they beheld the cause of the trouble.
2. He advanced, *followed by the five faithful workmen.*
3. *Having finished the work,* he demanded his pay.

EXERCISE 133

In the following sentences point out the prepositional, the infinitive, and the participial phrases, and tell by what each phrase is introduced : —

1. Strive to be usefully employed.
2. Having obtained the information, he ceased questioning.
3. They saw a small vessel approaching the shore.
4. At last, turning briskly away, she came toward the table.
5. We are anxious to learn the result.
6. He was unable to convince this man of his error.
7. Not one of these men offered to lend his assistance.
8. Down plunged the diver, and soon rose dripping from the water, holding the sea-shrub in his hand.
9. To love one's country has ever been esteemed honorable.
10.   And out again I curve and flow
        To join the brimming river.

EXERCISE 134

Write sentences containing (1) *a prepositional phrase used like an adjective;* (2) *a prepositional phrase used like an adverb;* (3) *a participial phrase used like an adjective;*

(4) *an infinitive phrase used as the subject of a verb;*
(5) *an infinitive phrase used as the object of a verb.*

II. CLASSIFICATION ACCORDING TO USE

State the office of each phrase in the following examples : —

1. The decision *of the judge* was just.
2. The house stands *on a high hill.*
3. *To defer action* will be unwise.
4. He refused *to open the gate.*

(1) **A phrase that performs the office of an adjective is an** *adjective phrase;* as, —

1. The doors *of the church* were open.
2. He beheld a stranger *standing near him.*
3. Listen to the song *of the bird.*

(2) **A phrase that performs the office of an adverb is an** *adverbial phrase;* as, —

1. They landed *on an island.*
2. He came *to inspect the work.*
3. The house stood *on this corner.*

(2) **A phrase that performs the office of a noun is a** *noun phrase;* as, —

1. *To please all* is impossible.
2. We hope *to hear the speaker.*

EXERCISE 135

Find the adjective, the adverbial, and the noun phrases in the following examples, and tell how each is used: —

1.   In happy homes he saw the light
   Of household fires gleam warm and bright.

2. Religion dwells not in the tongue, but in the heart.

3. Hark! I hear the bugles of the enemy.

4. A lamp was burning in the little chapel.

5. Rise with the lark.

6. It was one by the village clock.

7. The newly elected member went in state to the City Cross, accompanied by a band of music.

8. The doors of the prison closed upon him.

9. Around the walls stood several oak bookcases.

10. The edges and corners of the box were carved with most wonderful skill.

11. You must change your style of living.

12. Point thy tongue on the anvil of truth.

13. It stands on a mound which elevates it above the other parts of the castle, and a great flight of steps leads to the interior.

14. The paths of glory lead but to the grave.

15. Cease to do evil; learn to do well.

16.   Here delicate snow-stars, out of the cloud,
   Come floating downward in airy play.

EXERCISE 136

Write (1) *five sentences, each containing an adjective phrase;* (2) *five sentences, each containing an adverbial phrase;* (3) *two sentences, each containing a noun phrase.*

CHAPTER LXV

PREPOSITIONS

Tell what the following prepositions connect, and what relations they express: —

1. He stood *on* the bridge.
2. 'Twas the night *before* Christmas.
3. The tree was struck *by* lightning.
4. He died *for* his country.
5. The eyes *of* the sleepers waxed deadly and chill.

Prepositions express such a variety of relations that they cannot be easily classified according to meaning. The most common relations expressed by prepositions are —

(1) **Place** or **direction**; as, *At* home; *towards* the bridge; *below* the falls.

(2) **Time**; as, *After* breakfast; *till* noon; *since* morning.

(3) **Agency, instrumentality,** or **means**; as, Killed *by* frost; cut *with* a hatchet; lost *through* carelessness.

(4) **Cause** or **purpose**; as, Thankful *for* good health; he votes *from* principle.

(5) **Possession**; as, The voice *of* the speaker; the beauty *of* the rose; the blade *of* the knife.

(6) **Definition**; as, The virtue *of* temperance; the city *of* Rome.

(7) **Object**; as, The fear *of* death; the hope *of* reward.

Many other relations are implied, such as *reference*, expressed by *about;* *association*, by *with;* *separation*, by *from;* *opposition*, by *against;* *substitution*, by *for;* etc.

The words most commonly used as prepositions are the following : —

about	athwart	from	to
above	before	in	toward
across	behind	into	towards
after	below	of	under
against	beneath	off	underneath
along	beside	on	until
amid	besides	over	unto
amidst	between	round	up
among	beyond	since	upon
amongst	by	through	with
around	down	throughout	within
at	for	till	without

Concerning, during, notwithstanding, regarding, respecting touching, and a few similar words of participial form are usually classed as prepositions.

Certain phrases are used with the force of single prepositions. They are called compound prepositions; as, *according to, in place of, in regard to, instead of, out of, on account of.*

ORDER OF PARSING PREPOSITIONS

To parse a preposition, —

(1) Name the part of speech.

(2) Tell with what word it connects its object.

(3) State the relation shown.[1]

EXAMPLE. — He goes *on* Sunday *to* the church.

—LONGFELLOW.

[1] With young pupils, the third step may be omitted.

1. *On* is a preposition, connecting the noun *Sunday* with the verb *goes*, and showing the relation of time.

2. *To* is a preposition, connecting the noun *church* with the verb *goes*, and showing the relation of place.

EXERCISE 137

Parse the prepositions in the following sentences, and tell the use of each prepositional phrase: —

1. At midnight, however, I was aroused by the tramp of horses' hoofs in the yard.

2. Great turtles came up out of the water, and crawled along on a sandy place.—M. THOMPSON.

3. The scheme failed for want of support.

4.
> The love that leads the willing spheres
> Along the unending track of years
> And watches o'er the sparrow's nest,
> Shall brood above thy winter rest.—BRYANT.

5.
> With my cross-bow
> I shot the Albatross.—COLERIDGE.

6. The little bird sits at his door in the sun.—LOWELL.

7.
> On the cross-beam under the Old South bell
> The nest of a pigeon is builded well.
> In summer and winter that bird is there,
> Out and in with the morning air;
> I love to see him track the street,
> With his wary eye and active feet;
> And I often watch him as he springs,
> Circling the steeple with easy wings,
> Till across the dial his shade has passed,
> And the belfry edge is gained at last.—N. P. WILLIS.

CHAPTER LXVI

CLASSES OF CONJUNCTIONS

I. COÖRDINATING CONJUNCTIONS

Find in the following examples conjunctions that connect words, phrases, or clauses of like kind, or having the same relation to the rest of the sentence: —

1. Art is long, and time is fleeting.
2. Games and carols closed the day.
3. The house was silent and deserted.
4. You see where Warren fell, and where other patriots fell with him.

Words, phrases, and clauses of like kind, or standing in the same relation to the rest of the sentence, are said to have the same construction or to be of equal rank. **Conjunctions that connect words, phrases, or clauses of equal rank, are *coördinating conjunctions.*** They may connect —

(1) Two independent clauses; as, *Be diligent, **and** you will succeed.*

(2) Two words in the same construction; as, The minstrel was *infirm **and** old.*

(3) Two phrases in the same construction; as, They are alike *in voice **and** in manner.*

(4) Two dependent clauses in the same construction; as, No one could tell *whence they came **or** whither they went.*

Coördinating conjunctions are divided into the following classes: —

(1) **Copulative,** those that join similar parts; as, *and, also, besides, likewise, moreover.*

(2) **Adversative,** those that join parts opposed in meaning; as, *but, yet, however, still, nevertheless, notwithstanding.*

(3) **Alternative,** those that imply a choice between two; as, *either — or, neither — nor, whether — or.*

(4) **Causal,** those that express cause or consequence; as, *for, therefore, hence, consequently.*

Conjunctions used in pairs are called **correlatives;** as, *both — and, either—or, neither — nor, not — but, not only — but.*

EXERCISE 138

Point out the coördinating conjunctions in the following examples, and tell what they join: —

1. The shower was now over, and a rainbow above the eastern wood promised a fair evening.

2. Either he is talking, or he is pursuing.

3. Through days of sorrow and of mirth.

4. Be just, and fear not.

5. He calls on the people not only to defend, but to study and understand their rights and privileges.

6. This lesson is plain, and easily applied.

7. Their route now lay over rough ground, and their progress was slow.

8. He was interrupted by the flash and report of a rifle.

9. We know what we are, but know not what we may be.

10. The time we live ought not to be computed by the number of years, but by the use that has been made of them.

11. Virtuous and wise he was, yet not severe.

12. I know not whether to go or to remain.

13. He does not deserve to succeed; for he will not put forth effort.

14. Give me neither poverty nor riches.

15. He was small of stature, and slight in frame.

16. Read not to contradict, nor to believe, but to weigh and consider.

II. SUBORDINATING CONJUNCTIONS

Name the dependent clause in each of the following sentences, state its use, and tell how it is joined to the principal clause : —

1. I would grant your request if I could.
2. He came, because he was needed.
3. Be silent, that you may hear.

Conjunctions that connect a dependent or subordinate clause to a principal clause are *subordinating conjunctions.* They denote —

(1) **Time**; as, *after, before, ere, since, till, when, while, as.*

(2) **Place**; as, *where, whence.*

(3) **Manner** and **comparison**; as, *than, as.*

(4) **Cause** or **reason**; as, *because, since, as, that, whereas.*

(5) **End** or **purpose**; as, *that, lest.*

(6) **Condition**; as, *if, unless, except.*

(7) **Concession**; as, *though, although.*

Certain phrases performing the office of conjunctions may be called **compound conjunctions**; as, *but also, as well as, as if, as though.*

EXERCISE 139

Find the subordinating conjunctions in the following sentences, and tell what each denotes : —

1. I have not seen him since he was a child.
2. He labored earnestly that abuses might be reformed.
3. Love not sleep lest thou come to poverty.
4. Live well that you may die well.
5. His stories are good to hear at night, because we can dream about them asleep ; and good in the morning, too, because then we can dream about them awake.
6. Now had the season returned when the nights grow colder and longer.
7. A clownish air is but a small defect ; yet it is enough to make a man disagreeable.
8. Since we must fight it through, why not put ourselves in a state to enjoy all the benefit of victory, if we gain the victory.
9. A great black cloud had been gathering in the sky for some time past, although it had not overspread the sun.
10. Speak clearly, if you would be understood.

CHAPTER LXVII

HOW TO PARSE CONJUNCTIONS

To parse a conjunction, tell —

1. Its class — coördinating or subordinating.
2. Its use — state what it connects.

EXAMPLE I. — Hear me for my cause, *and* be silent, *that* you may hear.

1. *And* is a coördinating conjunction, connecting the two independent members, "Hear me for my cause," and "be silent, that you may hear."

2. *That* is a subordinating conjunction, connecting the subordinate clause, "you may hear," to the principal clause, "be silent."

EXAMPLE 2. — Is the night chilly *and* dark?

1. *And* is a coördinating conjunction, connecting the two adjectives *chilly* and *dark*.

EXERCISE 140

Parse the conjunctions in the following sentences: —

1.   My hair is gray, but not with years,
            Nor grew it white
            In a single night,
        As men's have grown from sudden fears:
        My limbs are bowed, though not with toil,
            But rusted with a vile repose,
        For they have been a dungeon's spoil,
            And mine has been the fate of those
        To whom the goodly earth and air
        Are banned, and barred, — forbidden fare. — BYRON.

2.   Here rests his head upon the lap of earth,
        A youth to fortune and to fame unknown. — GRAY.

3. They deserved respect; for they were good men as well as brave. — HAWTHORNE.

4.   On either side the river lie
        Long fields of barley and of rye. — TENNYSON.

5. Neither a borrower nor a lender be. — SHAKESPEARE.

6. As Cæsar loved me, I wept for him; as he was fortunate, I rejoice at it; as he was valiant, I honor him: but, as he was ambitious, I slew him. — SHAKESPEARE.

7. The test of a people is not in its occupations, but in its heroes. — T. W. HIGGINSON.

8.   Then they praised him, soft and low,
          Called him worthy to be loved,
       Truest friend and noblest foe;
          Yet she neither spoke nor moved. — TENNYSON.

9. One whole month elapsed before I knew the fate of the cargo.

10. The works of Milton cannot be comprehended or enjoyed, unless the mind of the reader coöperate with that of the writer. He does not paint a finished picture, or play for a mere passive listener. He sketches, and leaves others to fill up the outline. He strikes the key-note, and expects his hearer to make out the melody. — MACAULAY.

EXERCISE 141

REVIEW OF CONJUNCTIONS

Name the two leading classes of conjunctions. What is a coördinating conjunction? What is meant by words, phrases, or clauses of equal rank? Illustrate. Tell how coördinating conjunctions are classified, and give examples of each class.

What is a subordinating conjunction? Mention some of the different relations denoted by subordinating conjunctions, and give illustrations.

What are correlative conjunctions? Give examples.

Mention phrases that are used as conjunctions.

CHAPTER LXVIII

INTERJECTIONS

Since interjections are not grammatically related to the other words in a sentence, the parsing of an interjection consists in simply naming the part of speech.

EXERCISE 142

Name the interjections in the following sentences, and tell what feeling each expresses : —

1.   Ah ! what would the world be to us
        If the children were no more ? — LONGFELLOW.

2. Hark ! let me listen for the swell of the surf.

3. Ah ! what a weary race my feet have run. — WARTON.

4. Oh ! wherefore come ye forth, in triumph from the north ?
        — MACAULAY.

5. Alas ! I have nor hope nor health. — SHELLEY.

6. And, lo ! from far, as on they pressed, there came a glittering band. — HEMANS.

7. Hark ! hark ! the lark at heaven's gate sings.

8. Ha ! laugh'st thou, Lochiel, my vision to scorn ?

9.   For, lo ! the blazing, rocking roof
        Down, down in thunder falls ! — HORACE SMITH.

10.   Heigh ho ! daisies and buttercups,
        Fair yellow daffodils, stately and tall.

11.   O joy ! that in our embers
        Is something that doth live. — WORDSWORTH.

PART THIRD

———∘o◦❀◦o∘———

SYNTAX

Syntax treats of the grammatical relations of words in sentences. The relation that any part of speech bears to other parts of speech in the same sentence is called its **syntax** or **construction**.

CHAPTER LXIX

CONSTRUCTION OF NOUNS

I. NOMINATIVE CASE

Subject Nominative

(1) The *subject* of a verb is in the *nominative case;* as, — *Man* is mortal. *I* sprang to the stirrup.

EXERCISE 143

Find the subject nominatives in the following examples, and tell of what verb each is a subject : —

1. The fleet consisted of nine vessels.
2. Up flew the windows all.
3. Facts always yield the place of honor in conversation, to thoughts about facts.
4. Not a ripple stirred on the glassy surface of the lake.

5.   Somewhat back from the village street
Stands the old-fashioned country-seat.
Across its antique portico
Tall poplar-trees their shadows throw;
And from its station in the hall
An ancient timepiece says to all, —
        " Forever — never !
          Never — forever ! " — LONGFELLOW.

Predicate Nominative

(2) **A noun or pronoun used to complete the predicate after certain intransitive verbs, such as** *be, become, appear, look,* **and** *seem,* **and after the passive forms of a few transitive verbs like** *make, call, choose,* **and** *elect* **is in the** *nominative case;* as, —

Webster was a *statesman.*   He was elected *senator.*

The noun that completes the predicate in this manner refers to the same person or thing as the subject of the verb, and is in the same case as the word explained.   It is called a **predicate noun** or a **predicate nominative.**[1]

Infinitives and participles of verbs of the class just named take the same case after them as before them, when both nouns or pronouns denote the same person or thing; as, —

It was thought to be *he.*   We asked *him* to be our *leader.*
He, being a *foreigner,* was ineligible to office.

---

[1] The noun or adjective that completes the predicate in this manner is sometimes called an *attribute complement.*

EXERCISE 144

Parse the nouns in the following examples, and tell to what each predicate nominative refers : —

1. Every man's task is his life-preserver.
2. I am monarch of all I survey.
3.   Our fortress is the good greenwood,
              Our tent the cypress-tree.

4. Toil is the condition of our being.
5. The colonists were now no longer freemen ; they were entirely dependent on the King's pleasure.
6. He was one of the ablest seamen of his time, and was a favorite with his sailors.
7. Every day is a little life ; and our whole life is but a day repeated.
8. Each tree is an individual and has a personal character.

Apposition

A noun or pronoun added to another noun or pronoun to explain its meaning is called an **appositive,** or is said to be in **apposition** with the word explained.

(3) **An appositive is in the same case as the word explained;** as, —

Motley, the *historian*, was an American.   (Nominative case.)
We met your brother, the *general*.   (Objective case.)
Have you seen Gibson, the *artist's*,[1] drawings?   (Possessive case.)

[1] See page 50.

EXERCISE 145

Find the appositives in the following examples, state the case of each, and tell why it is in that case: —

1. Spenser, the poet, lived in the time of Queen Elizabeth.

2. The tiger, an animal equal to the lion in size, is a native of Asia.

3. He went to his old resort, the village inn.

4.   These gay idlers, the butterflies,
           Broke, to-day, from their winter shroud.

5. Samuel Adams, the distinguished patriot, died in 1803.

6. An ancient clock, that important article of cottage furniture, ticked on the opposite side of the room.

7.   The harp, his sole remaining joy,
           Was carried by an orphan boy.

8. My friend, Sir Roger, being a good churchman, has beautified the inside of his church with several texts of his own choosing.

Nominative Absolute

(4) **A noun or pronoun** used absolutely with a participle, its case not depending upon any other word, is in the *nominative case absolute;* as, —

The *fog* being very dense, we could not safely proceed.
The mountains rose, *peak* [being] above peak.

EXERCISE 146

Name the nouns and the pronouns that are in the nominative absolute, and tell with what participle, expressed or understood, each is used: —

1. The storm having ceased, the ships sailed.

2. Paul preached and taught with all confidence, no man forbidding him.

3. His calling laid aside, he lived at ease.

4. The supper being over, the strangers requested to be shown to their place of repose.

5.   But the lark is so brimful of gladness and love
     The green fields below him, the blue sky above.

                                        — COLERIDGE.

Nominative of Address

(5) **A noun used to name a person or thing addressed is in the *nominative case* of *address;* as, —**

> *Watchman,* tell us of the night.
> O *grave,* where is thy victory?

EXERCISE 147

Parse in full the nouns that are in the nominative of address : —

1. O Father ! I hear the sound of guns.

2. The fault, dear Brutus, is not in our stars,
   But in ourselves, that we are underlings. — SHAKESPEARE.

3. Veterans ! you are the remnant of many a well-fought field. — WEBSTER.

4. Oh Life ! I breathe thee in the breeze. — BRYANT.

5. Good friends, sweet friends, let me not stir you up to such a sudden flood of mutiny. — SHAKESPEARE.

EXERCISE 148

Write sentences illustrating five different constructions of a noun in the nominative case.

II. POSSESSIVE CASE

Possessive Modifier

A noun or pronoun used as a possessive modifier is in the *possessive case;* as, —

A friend should bear his *friend's* infirmities.

The noun denoting the thing possessed is sometimes omitted; as, —

Our first visit in Rome was to *St. Peter's.*

When two nouns in the possessive case are in apposition, only the noun immediately preceding the modified term, expressed or understood, takes the possessive sign; as, —

For thy servant *David's* sake.
For the *queen's* sake, his sister. — BYRON.

EXERCISE 149

Parse the nouns in the following examples: —

1. The village was two days' journey from the sea.

2. Buckingham Palace fronts on St. James's Park.

3. Let all the ends thou aim'st at be thy country's, thy God's, and truth's. — SHAKESPEARE.

4. At a little distance from Sir Roger's house, among the ruins of an old abbey, there is a long walk of aged elms, which are shot up so very high, that, when one passes under them, the rooks and crows that rest upon the tops of them seem to be cawing in another region. — ADDISON.

5. There, where a few torn shrubs the place disclose,
The village preacher's modest mansion rose. — GOLDSMITH.

6. We have no bird whose song will match the nightingale's in compass, none whose note is so rich as that of the European blackbird ; but for mere rapture I have never heard the bobolink's rival. — LOWELL.

III. OBJECTIVE CASE

Direct Object

(1) **A noun or pronoun used as the direct object** [1] **of a transitive verb (or of its participles or infinitives) is in the** *objective case ;* as, —

> Choose the *timbers* with greatest care.
> The pillars supporting the *roof* are strong.
> I come to bury *Cæsar*, not to praise *him*.

EXERCISE 150

Find in the following examples the nouns and the pronouns that are used as direct objects, and tell of what each is the object : —

1. One of the favorite themes of boasting with the Squire, is the noble trees on his estate, which, in truth, has some of the finest that I have seen in England.   There is something august and solemn in the great avenues of stately oaks that gather their branches together high in air, and seem to reduce the pedestrians beneath them to mere pygmies.   "An avenue of oaks or elms," the Squire observes, "is the true colonnade that should lead to a gentleman's house.   As to stone and marble, any one can rear them at once — they are the work of the day ; but commend me to the colonnades that have grown old and great with the family, and tell by their grandeur how long the family has endured." . . .

[1] See page 46.

It is with great difficulty that the Squire can ever be brought to have any tree cut down on his estate.   To some he looks with reverence, as having been planted by his ancestors ; to others with a kind of paternal affection, as having been planted by himself ; and he feels a degree of awe in bringing down, with a few strokes of the axe, what it has cost centuries to build up. — IRVING, Bracebridge Hall.

Object of Preposition

(2) **A noun or pronoun used as the object**[1] **of a preposition is in the *objective case ;*** as, —

> We spoke not a word of *sorrow.*
> Come with *me.*

EXERCISE 151

Select the objects of the prepositions in the following selection, and tell to what words they are joined by the prepositions : —

> Shut in from all the world without,
> We sat the clean-winged hearth about,
> Content to let the north-wind roar
> In baffled rage at pane and door,
> While the red logs before us beat
> The frost-line back with tropic heat ;
> And ever, when a louder blast
> Shook beam and rafter as it passed,
> The merrier up its roaring draught
> The great throat of the chimney laughed,
> The house-dog on his paws outspread
> Laid to the fire his drowsy head,
> The cat's dark silhouette on the wall
> A couchant tiger's seemed to fall ;

[1] See page 18.

And, for the winter fireside meet,
Between the andirons' straddling feet,
The mug of cider simmered slow,
The apples sputtered in a row,
And, close at hand, the basket stood
With nuts from brown October's wood.

— WHITTIER, Snow-Bound.

Indirect Object

(3) **A noun or pronoun used as an indirect object to show to whom or for whom or what something is done is in the** *objective* **(or dative)** *case ;* as, —

He gave the *man* [indirect object] a *coat* [direct object] (= He gave a coat *to* the man).

She bought the *bird* [indirect object] a *cage* [direct object] (= She bought a cage *for* the bird).

Usually the indirect object alone is used when the noun stands next the verb, the preposition when the noun is separated from the verb.

EXERCISE 152

Tell which verbs in the following sentences take two objects, and name the direct and the indirect object in each case : —

1. Give every man thy ear, but few thy voice.

2.   Then give him, for a soldier meet,
        A soldier's cloak for winding-sheet.

3. The sand ridge ran for a long way back into the swamp, and thus gave me a safe and easy road to the heart of a typical jungle.

4. I thrice presented him a kingly crown.

5. He giveth His beloved sleep.

6. Build thee more stately mansions, O my soul.

7. I made me great works; I builded me homes; I planted me vineyards.

8. Friends, Romans, countrymen, lend me your ears.

Objective Predicate

(4) **A noun used as an objective predicate is in the *objective case;*** as, —

They made him *secretary.*

An objective predicate, as in the example above, completes the meaning of a transitive verb, and describes its object. When the verbs *make, appoint, elect, call, choose,* and others of similar meaning, take a complement which describes the direct object of the verb, they are said to be **factitive,** and the complement is often called the *factitive object.* When verbs of this class are used in the passive voice, they are followed by the predicate nominative. (See page 182); as, —

He will be made *secretary.*

EXERCISE 153

Select the objective predicates in the following examples, tell what verb each completes, and what it describes : —

1. They made me queen of the May.

2. Few men make themselves masters of things they write or speak.

3. One touch of nature makes the whole world kin.

4. And Simon he surnamed Peter.

5. Time makes the worst enemies friends.

6. And God called the light Day, and the darkness he called Night.

Adverbial Objective

(5) **A noun used adverbially to modify a verb, an adjective, or an adverb, by denoting** *time, distance, weight, value,* **etc., is an** *adverbial object,* **and is said to be in the** *objective case, adverbially ;* as, —

> He held the office three *years*.
> The walk is three *feet* wide.
> Do not remain a *moment* longer.

EXERCISE 154

Find the adverbial objects, and tell what each modifies : —

1. An hour they sat in counsel. — BROWNING.

2. My little ones kissed me a thousand times o'er. — CAMPBELL.

3. I therefore walked back by the horseway, which was five miles round. — GOLDSMITH.

4. So all night long the storm roared on. — WHITTIER.

5. And a good south wind sprung up behind ;
    The Albatross did follow,
    And every day, for food or play,
    Came to the mariner's hollo ! — COLERIDGE.

Cognate Objective

Some verbs are followed by a noun which repeats the meaning of the verb. This is called a **cognate object**; as, —

> I *dreamed* a *dream*.   I *ran* a *race*.

(6) **A noun** used as a cognate object is in the *objective case*.

Name the cognate objectives in the following examples. and tell how each is used: —

1. I have fought a good fight.
2. Behold, I dream a dream of good.
3. He sleeps the sleep of the just.
4. Let me die the death of the righteous.
5. Well hast thou fought the better fight.

REVIEW OF CONSTRUCTION OF NOUNS

Write sentences illustrating six different constructions of a noun in the objective case.

State the construction of each italicized word in the following selection: —

For my part, I was always a *bungler* at all kinds of sport that required either *patience* or adroitness, and had not angled above half an *hour*, before I had completely "satisfied the sentiment," and convinced myself of the truth of Izaak Walton's *opinion*, that *angling* is *something* like poetry — a man must be born to it. I hooked *myself* instead of the *fish;* tangled my line in every tree; lost my bait; broke my rod; until I gave up the *attempt* in despair, and passed the *day* under the trees, reading old Izaak; satisfied that it was his fascinating *vein* of honest simplicity and rural feeling that had bewitched me, and not the passion for angling.

My *companions*, however, were more persevering in their delusion. I have them at this *moment* before my eyes, stealing along the *border* of the brook, where it lay open to the day, or was merely fringed by shrubs and bushes. I see the *bittern* rising with hollow scream, as they break in upon his rarely-invaded haunt; the *king-fisher* watching them suspiciously from his dry tree that overhangs the deep black *mill-pond*, in the gorge of the hills; the *tortoise* letting himself slip sideways from off the *stone* or log on which he is sunning himself; and the panic-struck *frog* plumping in headlong as they approach, and spreading an *alarm* throughout the watery *world* around. — IRVING, The Sketch-Book.

CHAPTER LXX

CONSTRUCTION OF PRONOUNS

I. AGREEMENT WITH ANTECEDENT

A pronoun must agree with its antecedent in person, number, and gender.

Antecedents modified by *each*, *every*, and *no* are singular; as, —

> Every tree is known by *its* fruit.

When reference is made to an antecedent that may denote a person of either sex, the pronoun of the masculine gender is generally used; as, —

> Each contributed what *he* could.

When the antecedent is a collective noun, it is neuter, and singular if reference is made to the collection as a whole, but plural if reference is made to the individuals in the collection separately ; as, —

> The army proceeded on *its* march.
> The army left *their* camp utensils behind *them*.

EXERCISE 158

Copy the following sentences, filling the blanks with suitable pronouns. Give in each case a reason for your choice : —

1. The committee decided the matter without leaving —— seats.
2. All passengers must show —— tickets.
3. Every passenger must show —— ticket.
4. Somebody left —— umbrella.
5. Men at some time are masters of —— fate.
6. Neither would admit that —— was in the wrong.
7. Each soldier carried —— own gun.
8.
> Happy, thrice happy, every one
> Who sees —— labor well begun.
9. One who would succeed must learn to think for ——.
10. The committee has offered to refund the amount which —— received from the company.
11. Every man must bear —— own burden.
12. The soldiers paused on —— march.

EXERCISE 159

State the person, number, and gender of each italicized pronoun in the following examples, giving reasons for your statements : —

1. The house stood among flourishing apple-trees, three or four of *which* are yet standing.

2. Every opinion reacts on him who utters it.

3. He *who* thinks much of himself will be in danger of being forgotten by the rest of the world.

4. He was surrounded by a shouting multitude, most of *whom* had been born in the country *which* he had helped to found.

5. So the Deacon inquired of the village folk
   Where he could find the strongest oak,
   That couldn't be split nor bent nor broke. — O. W. HOLMES.

6. Few, few were they *whose* swords of old
   Won the fair land in *which* we dwell. — BRYANT.

7. That is a good book which is opened with expectation, and closed with profit.

8.   Thou art Freedom's now, and Fame's,
             One of the few, the immortal names,
             That were not born to die. — HALLECK.

II. CASE RELATIONS OF THE PRONOUN

The case relations of the pronoun are nearly the same as those of the noun.

EXERCISE 160

State the case of each italicized pronoun in the following examples, and tell why it is in that case:—

I. Subject Nominative

1. *Who*, of all *that* address the public ear, whether in church, or court-house, or hall of state, has such an attentive audience as the town-crier?

2. *Few* believed the report.
3. *They that* have done this deed are honorable.
4. *What* caused the trouble?

II. Predicate Nominative

5. It is *I;* be not afraid.
6. All mine are *thine*, and thine are *mine*.
7. *Who* do men say that I am?

III. Apposition

8. We *all* do fade as a leaf.
9. They love *each* other.
10. The singer, *she* whom you most wished to hear, is ill.
11. I *myself* was surprised at the result.

IV. Nominative Absolute

12. *He* being absent, no one would discuss the question.
13. *Thou* looking on, I shall not fail.

V. Nominative of Address

14.   *Thou*, who wouldst see the lovely and the wild
Mingled in harmony on Nature's face,
Ascend our rocky mountains.

15. O *thou* that hearest prayer, unto thee shall all flesh come.

VI. Possessive Modifier

16.   And they *whose* meadows it murmurs through,
Have named the stream from *its* own fair hue.

17.   Two robin redbreasts built *their* nest
Within a hollow tree.

VII. Direct Object

18. No one heard *him*.
19. Seeing *me*, the bird flew.
20. We expect to meet *them*.

VIII. Object of Preposition

21. What to *me* is fame?
22. I that speak unto *thee* am he.
23. Stay, lady, stay with *us*.
24. *Whom* did you speak to?

IX. Indirect Object

25. Give *us* this day our daily bread.
26. Pay *me* that thou owest.
27. *Me*thinks I hear a step.[1]

III. NOMINATIVE AND OBJECTIVE FORMS

EXERCISE 161

Copy the following sentences, inserting the proper form of pronoun in each blank. Give in each case a reason for your choice:—

I, Me

1. She and —— found the nest.
2. He or —— will deliver your message.
3. Between you and ——, it was an unwise step.
4. The books were sent to him and ——.

---

[1] *Methinks* is an impersonal verb, made up of the pronoun *me* and the verb *think* (from an old verb meaning to seem or appear). The pronoun *me*, when combined in this manner with the verb *think* or *seem*, is an indirect object. The sentence above is equivalent to "It seems to me that I hear a step."

5. It was —— that opened the door.
6. Who is there? ——.
7. Is it —— that you mean?
8. Robert is smaller than ——.
9. He is as strong as ——.
10. No one wishes you success more earnestly than ——.

We, Us

11. They were as unfortunate as ——.
12. It could not have been —— that you heard.
13. Let —— change our plans.
14. They have greater responsibilities than ——.

Thou, Thee

15. —— art the man.
16. Gray-headed shepherd, —— hast spoken well.
17.
>   My country, 'tis of ——,
>   Sweet land of liberty,
>   Of —— I sing.

He, Him

18. Is —— coming?
19. If I were ——, I should not go.
20. I that speak to thee am ——.
21. You know as well as —— that this work should be done.
22. Will you go with —— and me?

She, Her

23. —— and I will assist you.
24. Did you say it was ——?
25. We asked —— to accompany us.
26. The flowers were given to —— and me.
27. Was it —— that you wished to see?

They, Them

28. Could it have been —— that called?
29. Let —— do the work in their own way.
30. No two are better fitted for the task than ——.
31. Arrange the matter between you and ——.

Who, Whom

32. —— did you meet?
33. —— rang the bell?
34. —— do you wish to see?
35. —— is it that you wish to see?
36. —— do you think will be chosen?
37. Do you know —— I am?
38. I am he —— you seek.
39. I do not know —— will go.
40. I cannot tell —— to send.
41. It was the secretary —— wrote the letter.
42. It was the President —— they asked to speak.

CHAPTER LXXI

CONSTRUCTION OF ADJECTIVES

I. USES OF THE ADJECTIVE

Which adjectives in the following sentences modify nouns directly, and which modify a noun or a pronoun through the verb? —

1. A soft answer turneth away wrath.
2. Ring out, wild bells.
3. The sky is clear.
4. He painted the house white.
5. Her beauty made me glad.

I. An adjective that modifies a noun or a pronoun directly is said to be used **attributively**; as, —

> *Drowsy* tinklings lull the *distant* fold.

II. An adjective loosely attached to its noun is said to be used **appositively**; as, —

> No misfortune, *public* or *private*, could oppress him.

III. An adjective that completes the predicate, and shows what is asserted of the subject of the verb, or describes the object of the verb, is called a **predicate adjective,** or is said to be used **predicatively**; as, —

> Snow is *white*.
> They set the prisoner *free*.

In poetry an adjective is sometimes used for an adverb; as, —

> *Silent* rows the gondolier.

EXERCISE 162

Tell how each adjective is used in the following sentences : —

1. The lamps shone o'er fair women and brave men.

2. Is it where the feathery palm-trees rise,
   And the date grows ripe under sunny skies?
   Or 'midst the green islands of glittering seas,
   Where fragrant forests perfume the breeze?

3. The fields were green, and the sky was blue. —SOUTHEY.

4.   The sea is mighty, but a mightier sways
   His restless billows. —BRYANT.

5. He wrapped her warm in his seaman's coat.

6. My keepers grew compassionate.

7. Besides, our losses have made us thrifty.

8. A single sentinel was pacing to and fro beneath the arched gateway which leads to the interior, and his measured footsteps were the only sound that broke the breathless silence of the night.

9. His faithful dog shall bear him company.

EXERCISE 163

(1) *Write four sentences containing adjectives used attributively.*

(2) *Write three sentences containing adjectives used predicatively, with intransitive verbs.*

(3) *Write three sentences containing adjectives used predicatively, with transitive verbs.*

II. AGREEMENT WITH NOUN

Adjectives denoting one, modify nouns in the singular; those denoting more than one, modify nouns in the plural.

EXERCISE 164

Justify the use of the italicized forms in the following examples : —

1. *That* kind of exercise does no good.
2. *This* sort of trees is excellent for shade.
3. *These* trees are too near together.
4. *This* style of chairs is not pleasing.
5. *These* chairs are not comfortable.
6. *That* sort of people will always make trouble.
7. Have you examined *those* books?
8. Books of *that* class are very helpful.

III. COMPARATIVE AND SUPERLATIVE FORMS

The comparative degree is used in comparing two things or classes of things ; as, —

> James is *taller* than William.
>
> Silver is *harder* than gold.

The superlative degree is used in comparing one thing with all others of the same kind ; as, —

> James is the *tallest* boy in his class.

When the comparative degree is used, the latter term of comparison should exclude the former; as, —

> *Africa* is *hotter* than *any other continent.*

When the superlative is used, the latter term should include the former; as, —

> *Africa* is the *hottest of the continents.*

EXERCISE 165

Re-write the following sentences, inserting the preferred form : —

1. He is the (wiser, wisest) of the two.
2. This design is the (better, best) of the three.
3. The crocodile is larger than (any, any other) reptile.
4. The crocodile is the largest of (all, all other) reptiles.
5. The white oak has a wider spread than (any, any other) American tree.
6. The pine contains a greater quantity of turpentine than (any, any other) family of resinous trees.
7. Of all the poets called Lake Poets, Wordsworth was the (greater, greatest).

CHAPTER LXXII

CONSTRUCTION OF VERBS

I. AGREEMENT WITH SUBJECT

What determines the person and number forms of the italicized verbs in the following sentences? —

1. The stream *flows* swiftly.
2. Thou *art* the man.
3. The new members *were* present.

When the form of the subject determines the form of the verb, a verb is said to *agree* with its subject. Hence the statement —

A verb must agree with its subject in person and number; as, —

I *am*.　　Thou *art*.　　He *is*.　　We *are*.

Some subjects plural in form are singular in meaning and take verbs in the singular; as, —

The news is delayed.
"Twice-Told Tales" *was* written by Hawthorne.

A collective noun requires a verb in the singular when it denotes the collection as a whole, and a verb in the plural when it denotes the individuals in the collection separately; as, —

The congregation *was* dismissed.
The whole congregation *were* in tears.

Two or more subjects in the singular connected by *and* require a verb in the plural; as, —

> *Time* and *tide* wait for no man.

If the subjects refer to the same person or thing or express one idea, the verb must be singular; as, —

> The soldier and statesman *has* passed away.
> The horse and carriage *is* at the door.
> Two years *seems* like a long time.

When the subjects are preceded by *each*, *every*, or *no*, they refer to things considered separately, and require a verb in the singular; as, —

> Each day and each hour *brings* its duties.

Two or more subjects in the singular connected by *or*, *either* ... *or*, or *neither* ... *nor*, require a verb in the singular; as, —

> He or she *was* in the wrong.
> Neither he nor she *is* present.

When a verb has two or more subjects of different persons connected by *or* or *nor*, it is generally made to agree in person and number with the subject nearest to it; as, —

> Either *he* or *I have* made a mistake.
> *You* or *he is* right.

Or, better, the construction of the sentence may be changed. Thus —

> Either he *has* made a mistake or I *have*.
> You *are* right or he *is*.

EXERCISE 166

State the person and the number of each italicized verb in the following sentence, and tell why these forms are used: —

1. The difficulties *were* all over now, and everything *was* settled.

2. A little fire *is* quickly trodden out.

3. Delicacy and brilliancy *characterize* nearly all the California flowers.

4. The derivation of these words *is* uncertain.

5. It is an ill wind that *blows* nobody good.

6. Neither the secretary nor the treasurer *was* present.

7. The army is *needed* for the defence of the country.

8. How *does* such a loose pile of sticks maintain its place during a heavy wind?

9. A hundred eager fancies and busy hopes *keep* him awake.

10. The council *were* divided in their opinions.

11. Slow and sure *comes* up the golden year.

12. Either ability or inclination *was* wanting.

13. Let us hold fast the great truth that the people *are* responsible.

14. A word or an epithet *paints* a whole scene.

15. The saint, the father, and the husband *prays*. — BURNS.

16. Seasons *return*, but not to me *returns*
    Day, or the sweet approach of even or morn. — MILTON.

EXERCISE 167

(1) *Write three sentences in each of which the verb has two or more singular subjects connected by* **and.**

(2) *Write three sentences in each of which the verb has two or more singular subjects connected by* **or** *or* **nor.**

(3) *Write two sentences in each of which the subject is a collective noun denoting the collection as a whole.*

(4) *Write two sentences in each of which the subject is a collective noun denoting the individuals in the collection separately.*

II. SEQUENCE OF TENSES

The tense forms of verbs in subordinate clauses must correspond to the tense forms used in the principal clauses; as, —

> I *hope* you *can* come.
> I *hoped* you *could* come.
> He *does* this that you *may* see.
> He *did* this that you *might* see.
> He *says* that the work *shall* be done.
> He *said* that the work *should* be done.

Verbs like *hope, expect, intend*, referring to future acts, are followed by the present infinitive; as, —

> I intended *to visit* the museum.
> We expected *to remain* longer.
> I had intended *to visit* the museum.
> We had expected *to remain* longer.

EXERCISE 168

Justify the use of the italicized tense forms in the following examples : —

1. She walks that she *may* retain her health.
2. He will tell you that he *will* do his best.
3. He said that he *would* give an early reply.
4. We have done no more than it was our duty *to do*.
5. They expected *to see* us.

6. She seemed *to feel* the motion of the vessel.
7. He appeared *to have seen* better days.
8. I am glad *to have met* you.
9. I hoped *to meet* you.
10. He meant *to finish* the sketch.

CHAPTER LXXIII

CONSTRUCTION OF INFINITIVES

The chief constructions of the infinitives, including those already given, are the following : —

I. The simple infinitive, without **to,** is used after the verbs, *may*, *can*, *must*, *dare*, etc. ; as, —

Men must *work*.

II. Both the infinitive with **to** and the infinitive in -**ing** may be used, like a noun —

(1) As the **subject of a verb ;** as, —

To see is to believe.
Seeing is believing.

(2) As a **predicate nominative ;** as, —

To hesitate is *to fail.*
Begging is not *serving*.

(3) As the **object of a transitive verb ;** as, —

We propose *to call* a meeting.
We propose *calling* a meeting.

(4) As the **object of a preposition.**

She was about *to speak*.
On *reaching* the door, he paused.

III. The infinitive with **to** is used —

(1) As an **adjective modifier**; as, —

> There is a time *to weep*.

(2) As an **adverbial modifier**; as, —

> Strive *to excel*.
> She is eager *to go*.
> He is old enough *to know* better.

(3) To express **purpose**, consequence, etc.; as, —

> He came *to assist* his comrades.

(4) **Elliptically** or **absolutely**; as, —

> He was petrified, so *to speak*.
> *To tell* the truth, I do not believe it.

IV. The infinitive, usually with **to**, is used with a noun or a pronoun as the **object** of a **verb**; as, —

> He ordered the *troops to advance*.
> I asked *him to sing*.

In this construction, the noun or the pronoun which is used with the infinitive as the object of the verb is called the **subject** of the **infinitive**. The subject of an infinitive is in the objective case.

A few simple verbs, such as *let*, *hear*, *make*, *see*, etc., take in this construction the simple infinitive; as, Let me *go;* I saw him *fall*.

V. The infinitive in -ing, like the noun, takes a **possessive noun** or **pronoun**; as, —

Much depends on *Robert's receiving* the message.

His coming was not unexpected.

EXERCISE 169

Point out the infinitives in the following sentences, and state the construction of each: —

1. For him, to hear is to obey.
2. A sower went forth to sow.
3. He taught her to see new beauties in nature. — IRVING.
4. I come not, friends, to steal away your hearts.
5. The sun is just about to set. — TENNYSON.
6. And many a holy text around she strews
   That teach the rustic moralist to die. — GRAY.
7. She heard the birds sing, she
   Saw the sun shine. — LONGFELLOW.
8. After tarrying a few days in the bay, our voyagers weighed anchor, to explore a mighty river which emptied into the bay.
9. And fools who came to scoff remained to pray.
10. I did send to you for gold to pay my legions. — SHAKESPEARE.
11. Hast thou a charm to stay the morning star? — COLERIDGE.
12. Upon the landlord's leaving the room, I could not avoid expressing my concern for the stranger. — GOLDSMITH.
13. To live in hearts we leave behind
    Is not to die. — CAMPBELL.

EXERCISE 170

(1) *Write sentences illustrating two different uses of the simple infinitive without* **to**.

(2) *Write four sentences containing infinitives used like nouns.*

(3) *Write two sentences containing infinitives used like adjectives.*

(4) *Write three sentences containing infinitives used like adverbs.*

CHAPTER LXXIV

CONSTRUCTION OF PARTICIPLES

Participles modify nouns or pronouns. They may be used —

I. **Attributively**; as, —

> The *rising* sun hides the stars.

II. **Appositively**, usually equivalent to an implied clause; as, —

> Truth, *crushed* to earth, shall rise again.

III. **Predicatively**; as, —

> Here it runs *sparkling*. (Modifying the subject.)
> He kept us *waiting*. (Modifying the object.)

IV. **Absolutely**; as, —

> The service *having closed*, we left the church.

EXERCISE 171

Parse the participles and the infinitives in the following sentences : —

1. As we stood waiting on the platform, a telegraphic message was handed in silence to my companion. — HOLMES.

2. An uprooted tree came drifting along the current, and became entangled among the rocks.

3. "Ah!" cried he, drawing back in surprise.

4. The turban folded about his head
   Was daintily wrought of the palm-leaf braid.

5. At each corner of the building is an octagon tower, surmounted by a gilt ball and weathercock. — IRVING.

6. All the stories of ghosts and goblins that he had heard in the afternoon, now came crowding upon his recollection.

7. I saw you sitting in the house, and I no longer there.

8. The snow fell hissing in the brine,
   And the billows frothed like yeast. — LONGFELLOW.

9. Upon his advancing toward me with a whisper, I expected to hear some secret piece of news. — ADDISON.

10. A word fitly spoken is like apples of gold in pictures of silver. — BIBLE.

11. His father, being at the warehouse, did not yet know of the accident. — GEORGE ELIOT.

12. The wind having failed at sunset, the crew set to work with a will.

13. Here is a good place to test the qualities of a book as an out-door companion.

14. There is not wind enough to twirl
    The one red leaf, the last of its clan,
    That dances as often as dance it can,
    Hanging so light, and hanging so high,
    On the topmost twig that looks up at the sky. — COLERIDGE.

15. The talent of success is nothing more than doing what you can do, well. — LONGFELLOW.

16. To reverse the rod, to spell the charm backward, to break the ties which bound a stupefied people to the seat of enchantment, was the noble aim of Milton. — MACAULAY.

CHAPTER LXXV

CONSTRUCTION OF ADVERBS

I. POSITION OF ADVERBS

An adverb should be so placed that there can be no doubt as to its relation to the rest of the sentence ; as, —

> We were *greatly* surprised at the result.
> I saw *only* two trees in the yard.

An adverb should not be placed between *to*, the sign of an infinitive, and the infinitive itself, unless this arrangement would add to the clearness or the effectiveness of the sentence.

EXERCISE 172

Read the following sentences, inserting the words from the parentheses. Be careful to place each word so that it will express the meaning intended : —

1. The two houses were alike (nearly).
2. I will mention some of the best (only).
3. He promised to return (faithfully).
4. Tell him to leave the room (instantly).
5. There were two or three persons present (only).
6. I desired to go (really).
7. They remained three days (only).
8. We are directed to begin the work (immediately).
9. We came to look at the building (merely).

II. DOUBLE NEGATIVES

Two negatives should not be used in the same sentence, unless we wish to make an affirmation ; as, —

He can *not* do anything, or He can do *nothing* (not He can *not* do *nothing*).

Sometimes two negatives are used to make an affirmative; as, —

He is *not* *un*fitted for the position.

EXERCISE 173

Point out the negatives in the following examples, and tell which sentences are affirmative and which negative: —

1. I can do nothing for you.
2. He will never consent to the sale of the house.
3. I have received no information on the subject.
4. Neither he nor any one else can do that.
5. He is not unhappy.
6. She will not admit that she was wrong.
7. Neither you nor anybody else can change the facts.
8. I am not unmindful of my privileges.

CHAPTER LXXVI

CONSTRUCTION OF PREPOSITIONS

I. PREPOSITIONS DISCRIMINATED

Certain prepositions have distinctive uses.   Thus —

At is used before the name of a city or a town when the place is regarded merely as a point of locality; *in*, when reference is made to presence within its limits.   *In* is used before the names of countries.

At means in or near a place; *to* implies motion.

Beside denotes by the side of; *besides*, in addition to.

Between is ordinarily used in speaking of two things or classes of things; *among* in speaking of more than two.

By refers to the agent; *with*, to the instrument or means.

In denotes presence inside of; *into*, entrance from the outside to the inside.

EXERCISE 174

Copy the following sentences, filling the blanks with prepositions that will express the relation intended: —

At, In

1. The American poet, Longfellow, was born —— Portland, Maine.
2. The travellers landed —— Liverpool.
3. They are spending the winter —— London.
4. Shakespeare is buried —— Stratford Church —— Stratford-on-Avon.
5. Gold was discovered —— California in 1848.

At, To

6. Did you find him —— home?
7. He had gone —— New York.
8. She would stay —— home.
9. He went —— the hotel.
10. I saw him —— the hotel.

Beside, Besides

11. I sat —— the glowing grate.
12. —— the house, he offered us the use of the furniture.

13. The lady sat down —— the child.
14. Only three persons entered the cave —— the guide.
15. He stood —— the fountain.
16. There were six boys —— Herbert.

Between, Among

17. A small table stands —— the two windows.
18. The garments were distributed —— forty children.
19. He was a great favorite —— all the children of the village.
20. The birds were hopping and twittering —— the bushes.
21. The nest was —— two branches of an apple-tree.

By, With

22. The soil was prepared —— the gardener —— his spade.
23. Two houses were struck —— lightning.
24. Many of the early settlers were killed —— unseen foes.
25. The bill was signed —— this pen.
26. The wall was undermined —— frost.
27. The house was entered —— a burglar —— a skeleton key.

In, Into

28. The bobolink places its nest —— the midst of a broad meadow.
29. There were five young birds —— the nest.
30. Come —— the house.
31. He dropped one oar —— the water.
32. The children are playing —— the park.
33. We were admitted —— a spacious picture-gallery.
34. The troops marched —— the city.
35. The sweet peas are coming up —— the garden.

II. SPECIAL PREPOSITIONS

Certain words and phrases are followed by special prepositions; as, —

Abhorrent *to*.
Absolve *from*.
Accord *with*.
Accuse *of*.
Agree *to* (a thing proposed).
Agree *with* (a person).
Angry *with* (a person).
Appropriate *to*.
Bound *for* or *to*.
Conform *to*.
Complain *of*.
Comply *with*.
Correspond *to* (a thing).
Correspond *with* (a person).
Deprive *of*.

Different *from*.
Difficulty *in*.
Disappointed *in* (what we have).
Dissent *from*.
Involve *in*.
Matter *with*.
Need *of*.
Opposition *to*.
Prevent *from*.
Similar *to*.
Taste *of* (what is actually enjoyed).
Taste *for* (what we have capacity for enjoying).

EXERCISE 175

Copy the following sentences, filling the blanks with appropriate prepositions: —

1. The ship is bound —— Malta.
2. My card is different —— yours.
3. The soldiers did not complain —— the food.
4. She feels the need —— rest.
5. What was the matter —— the child?
6. The furniture does not correspond —— the house.
7. I am greatly disappointed —— the portrait.
8. Do you correspond —— your brother?
9. How does this version accord —— yours!

10. It is best to comply —— the regulations.
11. Suppose they will not agree —— the proposal.
12. He had difficulty —— making up his mind.
13. She has no taste —— music.
14. This plan is similar —— yours.

•

CHAPTER LXXVII

CONSTRUCTION OF CONJUNCTIONS

CORRELATIVES

When conjunctions are used in pairs, the two words must correspond, and they must be placed in corresponding positions in the sentence.

Some of the most common correlatives are *both* followed by *and; either, or; neither, nor; though, yet; whether, or; as, as* (to express equality); *so, as* (to deny equality).

EXERCISE 176

Point out the correlatives in the following examples, and show that they join corresponding parts of the sentence: —

1. He studied art both in France and in Italy.
2. Though he was rich, yet for your sakes he became poor.
3. Neither despise the poor, nor envy the rich.
4. His raiment was as white as snow.
5. This print is not so clear as that.
6. I do not know whether to go or to remain.
7. Neither a borrower nor a lender be.
8. He is either careless or indifferent.

CHAPTER LXXVIII

VARIED USES OF WORDS

EXERCISE 177

Give a reason for the classification of each italicized word in the following examples :—

All

1. *All* men are mortal.   (Adjective.)
2. *All* joined in the song.   (Pronoun.)
3. My *all* is lost.   (Noun.)
4. I am *all* alone.   (Adverb.)

As

1. He wrote *as* (Adverb of Degree) well *as* (Conjunctive Adverb) he could.
2. *As* he was ambitious, I slew him.   (Conjunction.)
3. They chose him *as* a leader.   (Conjunction introducing an appositive word.)
4. We are such stuff *as* dreams are made of.   (Relative Pronoun.)

Before

1. She had not entered this hall *before*.   (Adverb.)
2. He stood *before* me.   (Preposition.)
3. Look *before* you leap.   (Conjunction.)

But

1. Fools admire, *but* men of sense approve.   (Conjunction.)
2. Nought is heard *but* [except] the lashing waves.   (Preposition.)

3. Man wants *but* [only] little here below.   (Adverb.)
4.   There is no fireside, howsoe'er defended,
               But has one vacant chair.   (Relative Pronoun.)

Else

1. Anybody *else* would consent.   (Adjective.)
2. Where *else* could he go?   (Adverb.)
3. I have no tears, *else* would I weep for thee.   (Conjunction.)

Enough

1. *Enough* is as good as a feast.   (Noun.)
2. They have books *enough*.   (Adjective.)
3. He has worked long *enough*.   (Adverb.)

Except

1. No one heard the alarm *except* me.   (Preposition.)
2. I will not let thee go, *except* thou bless me.   (Conjunction.)

For

1. We shall wait *for* the boat.   (Preposition.)
2. I called, *for* I was wild with fear.   (Conjunction.)

However

1. *However* busy he may be, he will aid you.   (Adverb.)
2. These conditions, *however*, he could not accept.   (Conjunction.)

Like

1. This box is *like* yours.   (Preposition.)
2. He ran *like* a deer.   (Preposition.)
3. I *like* to read.   (Verb.)

Since

1. I have not thought of the matter *since*. (Adverb.)
2. We have not heard of him *since* morning. (Preposition.)
3. *Since* the books are here, we will use them. (Conjunction.)

So

1. *So* ended the conflict. (Adverb.)
2. The library was closed, *so* we returned home. (Conjunction.)

That

1. *That* book is lost. (Adjective.)
2. *That* is the cause of the trouble. (Adjective Pronoun.)
3. Here is the man *that* gave the order. (Relative Pronoun.)

The

1. *The* way was long. (Adjective.)
2. *The* sooner, *the* better [= by *how much* sooner, by *so much* better. (Adverb of Degree.)

CHAPTER LXXIX

SELECTIONS FOR PARSING

EXERCISE 178

Parse the italicized words in the following exercises, giving a full explanation of the different constructions :—

Whoever *has made* a voyage *up* the Hudson, *must remember* the Kaatskill Mountains. *They* are a dismembered *branch* of the great *Appalachian family*, and *are seen away* to the west of the river, *swelling up* to a noble height, *and lording it over* the surrounding *country*. Every *change* of season, *every* change of *weather, indeed,* every *hour* of the day, *produces some* change in the magical *hues and* shapes of *these mountains; and* they *are regarded* by *all* the good *wives, far and near, as* perfect *barometers*. *When* the weather is *fair* and *settled,* they *are clothed* in *blue* and *purple,* and *print* their bold *outlines on* the clear evening sky ; *but sometimes, when* the *rest* of the *landscape is cloudless,* they *will gather* a *hood* of gray vapors *about* their summits, *which in* the last rays *of* the *setting* sun, *will glow* and *light up like* a *crown* of *glory.* —WASHINGTON IRVING.

EXERCISE 179

All the *inhabitants* of the little village are busy. *One is clearing* a *spot* on the verge *of* the forest *for* his homestead ; *another* is hewing the trunk of a *fallen pine-tree, in order to build himself* a *dwelling;* a third *is hoeing* in his field of Indian corn. *Here comes* a huntsman *out of* the woods, *dragging* a bear *which* he has shot, *and shouting* to the neighbors *to lend him* a hand. *There goes* a *man* to the *seashore, with* a spade *and* a bucket, *to dig* a mess of clams, *which* were a principal *article* of food with the first settlers. *Scattered here* and *there* are two *or* three dusky *figures, clad* in mantles *of* fur, with ornaments of bone *hanging* from *their* ears, and the feathers of *wild* birds in their *coal-black* hair. They have *belts* of shell-work *slung across* their shoulders, and are *armed* with bows and arrows and *flint-headed* spears. *These* are an Indian *sagamore* and his attendants, *who* have come *to gaze* at the labors of the white men. *And now rises* a *cry that* a *pack* of wolves *have seized* a young calf in the pasture ; and every man *snatches up* his gun or pike and *runs* in chase of the *marauding* beasts. — NATHANIEL HAWTHORNE.

Part Fourth

STRUCTURE AND ANALYSIS OF SENTENCES

——o•o••o——

CHAPTER LXXX

STRUCTURE OF THE SENTENCE

I. ELEMENTS OF A SENTENCE

A *sentence* is the expression of a complete thought in words.

The *elements* of a sentence are the words, phrases, or clauses of which it is made up.

According to rank, elements are principal, subordinate, or independent.

The *principal elements* of a sentence are the simple subject and the simple predicate [1]; as, —

The *spring comes* slowly up this way.

The *subordinate elements* of a sentence are the modifiers of the principal elements; as, —

The doors *of the prison* closed *upon him.*
He *that leans on his own strength* leans *on a broken reed.*

[1] See page 4.

When the predicate verb is of incomplete predication, the object or the complement may be called a modifier of the grammatical predicate; as, —

> The sexton rang *the bell*.
> My mirror is *the mountain spring*.

The *independent elements* of a sentence are the words or phrases not grammatically related to the other words in the sentence; as, —

> *O Father!* I hear the sound of guns.
> *Well*, were you successful in your search?
> *To tell the truth*, I was disappointed.

EXERCISE 180

Point out the principal, the subordinate, and the independent elements in the following examples: —

1. Hark, there is a knock at the door.
2. Once more he stept into the street.
3. Early next morning I went to visit the grounds.
4. The first light dry snow had fallen.
5. Deer-tracks were discovered on the trails leading to the river.
6. Many, alas! had fallen in battle.
7. To speak plainly, the plan can never succeed.
8. At any rate, we can make the attempt.
9. This little brook flowed under a wooden bridge.

II. STRUCTURE OF ELEMENTS

When the subject, the predicate, the object, or the complement consists of two or more connected terms of equal rank, it is said to be **compound**; as, —

> *Games* and *carols* closed the busy day.
> The rainbow *comes* and *goes.*
> Learn *to labor* and *to wait.*
> Her voice was *low* and *sweet.*

Modifiers may be **simple, compound,** or **complex.**
A modifier consisting of a single word or phrase is **simple.**

> The ship went *slowly.*
> We spoke not a word *of sorrow.*

A modifier consisting of two or more connected words or phrases is **compound;** as, —

> The ship went *slowly and smoothly.*
> His cohorts were gleaming *in purple and gold.*

A modifier consisting of a word or phrase with modifiers of its own is **complex;** as, —

> The ship went *very slowly.*
> Here rests his head *upon the lap of earth.*

A series of adjectives may form a compound or a complex modifier as, —

> 1. He was an *honest, temperate, forgiving* man.
> 2. *Two large elm* trees stood near the house.

In the first example the adjectives are coördinate, each modifying the same noun. Adjectives used in this manner may be separated by commas or joined by conjunctions.

In the second example the adjectives form a complex modifier. *Two* modifies the whole expression *large elm trees, large* modifies *elm trees,* and *elm* modifies *trees.*

EXERCISE 181

Point out the compound and the complex elements in the following examples, and state their use in the sentence: —

1. And now there came both mist and snow.
2. He was not to be corrupted either by titles or by money.
3. The dove found no rest for the sole of her foot.
4. An alarm bell rang loudly and hurriedly.
5. The star and crescent graced his shield.
6. Heart, lungs, and brain play on through all the thousand nights of sleep.
7. He is our help and our shield.
8. She heard the tramp of horses' hoofs and the rattling of wheels.
9. This ancient city was captured and burned.
10. The children march and sing.

III. CLASSES OF SENTENCES

(1) STRUCTURE OF SENTENCES

According to their structure, sentences are *simple, complex,* or *compound.*

A sentence that expresses one thought is a *simple sentence;* as, —

The march of the human mind is slow.

A sentence consisting of one principal clause and one or more subordinate clauses is a *complex sentence;* as, —

Some murmur when their sky is clear.

A sentence made up of two or more independent members is a *compound sentence*; as, —

> *I listened, but I could not hear.*

(2) Use of Sentences

According to their use, sentences are *declarative, imperative, interrogative*, or *exclamatory*.

A sentence that states or declares something is a *declarative sentence*; as, —

> *The troops marched steadily on.*

A sentence that expresses a command or an entreaty is an *imperative sentence*; as, —

> *Make a proper use of your time.*

A sentence that asks a question is an *interrogative sentence*; as, —

> *When will the ship sail?*

A sentence that expresses sudden or strong feeling is an *exclamatory sentence*; as, —

> *What a beautiful rose this is!*

EXERCISE 182

Write (1) *a simple declarative sentence;* (2) *a simple imperative sentence;* (3) *a simple interrogative sentence;* (4) *a simple exclamatory sentence;* (5) *a compound declarative sentence;* (6) *a complex interrogative sentence.*

CHAPTER LXXXI

THE SIMPLE SENTENCE

A simple sentence is a sentence that expresses one thought.

I. THE SUBJECT

The **subject** of a simple sentence may be —

I. A **noun**; as, —

> *Birds* have many enemies.

II. A **pronoun**; as, —

> *We* expected a different answer.

III. An **infinitive**, or an **infinitive phrase**; as, —

> *To delay* is dangerous.
> *To say nothing* is often better than to speak.
> *Saying nothing* is often better than speaking.

EXERCISE 183

Write (1) *a simple sentence with a noun as subject;* (2) *a simple sentence with a pronoun as subject;* (3) *a simple sentence with an infinitive phrase as subject.*

II. MODIFIERS OF THE SUBJECT

The **subject** may be **modified by** —

I. An **adjective**; as, —

> *Still* waters run deep.

II. A **noun** or a **pronoun** in the **possessive case;** as, —

> *Edward's* friends were present.
> *My* opinion is not changed.

III. An **appositive word** or **phrase.**

I, *Paul*, have written it with mine own hand.
Hope, *the balm of life*, soothes us under every misfortune.

IV. A **prepositional phrase,** as adjective; as, —

> The paths *of glory* lead but to the grave.

V. An **infinitive;** as, —

> His desire *to learn* is great.

VI. A **participle,** or a **participial phrase;** as, —

> *Having sung*, she left the room.
> *Advancing cautiously*, he opened the door.

EXERCISE 184

Write sentences illustrating five different kinds of modifiers of the subject.

III. THE PREDICATE

The **predicate** of a simple sentence may be

I. A complete **verb** —

(1) In a **simple form;** as, The sun *rose*.
(2) In a **compound form;** as, The sun *has risen*.

II. An incomplete **intransitive verb** completed by —

(1) A **noun**; as, He was *secretary*.

(2) A **pronoun**; as, It was *he*.

(3) An **adjective**; as, Iron is *hard*.

(4) An **infinitive**, or an **infinitive phrase**; as, To see is *to believe*. To see her is *to love her*.

III. An incomplete **transitive verb** with its **object** —

(1) A **noun**; as, I hear *music*.

(2) A **pronoun**; as, We saw *them*.

(3) An **infinitive**, or an **infinitive phrase**; as, She likes *to read*. She likes *to read* stories.

(4) Or **objects** — direct and indirect; as, He gave *John a book*.

(5) And **objective complement**; as, They made him *treasurer*. The heat turned the milk *sour*.

EXERCISE 185

Write sentences illustrating three different forms of predicate.

IV. MODIFIERS OF THE PREDICATE

The **predicate verb** may be **modified** by —

I. An **adverb**; as, —

The bells ring *merrily*.

II. A **prepositional phrase**, as adverb; as, —

He went *towards the river*.

III. An **infinitive**, or an **infinitive phrase**; as, —

They came *to see the paintings*.

IV. An **adverbial objective**; as, —

> She remained two *hours*.

V. A **nominative absolute phrase**; as, —

> *The war being ended*, the soldiers returned.

The phrase, "the war being ended," gives a reason for the return of the soldiers. It is an adverbial phrase, being nearly equivalent in meaning to the adverbial clause, "as the war was ended."

EXERCISE 186

Write sentences illustrating five different kinds of modifiers of the subject.

V. ANALYSIS OF SIMPLE SENTENCES

To analyze a simple sentence —

(1) Tell the kind of sentence.
(2) Name the subject and the predicate.
(3) Tell what the subject consists of.
(4) Tell what the predicate consists of.

EXAMPLE I. — This old ship had been laden with immense wealth.

ORAL ANALYSIS

1. This is a simple declarative sentence.

2. The complete subject is *this old ship;* the complete predicate, *had been laden with immense wealth.*

3. The subject consists of the noun *ship*, with the adjectives *this* and *old*, of which *old* modifies *ship*, and *this* modifies *old ship*.

4. The predicate consists of the verb *had been laden*, modified by the adverbial phrase *with immense wealth*.

WRITTEN ANALYSIS. — *Simple Declarative Sentence*

Complete Subject	This old ship
Simple Subject Modifiers	*Noun :* ship *Adjectives :* this, old
Complete Predicate	had been laden with immense wealth
Simple Predicate Modifier	*Verb :* had been laden *Adverbial phrase :* with immense wealth

EXAMPLE II. — The prospect of success seemed small.

ORAL ANALYSIS. — 1. This is a simple declarative sentence.

2. The complete subject is *the prospect of success;* the complete predicate, *seemed small.*

3. The subject consists of the noun *prospect,* modified by the adjective *the* and by the adjective phrase *of success.*

4. The predicate consists of the verb *seemed,* completed by the adjective *small.*

Complete Subject	The prospect of success
Simple Subject Modifiers	*Noun :* prospect *Adjective :* the *Adjective phrase :* of success
Complete Predicate	seemed small
Simple Predicate Complement	*Verb :* seemed (*incomplete*) *Adjective :* small

EXAMPLE III. — Having obtained the desired information, he left the room.

ORAL ANALYSIS

1. This is a simple declarative sentence.

2. The complete subject is *he having obtained the desired information;* the complete predicate, *left the room.*

3. The subject consists of the pronoun *he*, modified by the participial phrase, *having obtained the desired information.*

4. The predicate consists of the verb *left*, completed by the object *room*, which is modified by *the.*

WRITTEN ANALYSIS

Simple Declarative Sentence

Complete Subject	he, having obtained the desired information
Simple Subject Modifier	*Pronoun :* he *Adjective phrase :* having obtained the desired information
Complete Predicate	left the room
Simple Predicate Object	*Verb :* left (*incomplete*) *Noun with modifier :* the room

EXAMPLE IV. — It is useless to deny the fact.

ORAL ANALYSIS

1. This is a simple declarative sentence.

2. The grammatical subject is *it*, which stands for the logical subject, *to deny the fact;* the predicate, *is useless.*

3. The logical subject is the infinitive phrase, *to deny the fact*, placed after the verb.

4. The predicate consists of the verb *is*, completed by the adjective *useless*.

WRITTEN ANALYSIS

Simple Declarative Sentence

Logical Subject	To deny the fact
Gram. Subject	*Pronoun :* it
Complete Predicate	is useless
Simple Predicate Complement	*Verb :* is (*incomplete*) *Adjective :* useless

EXERCISE 187

Analyze the following sentences, according to the models given on pages 230 *and* 231 : —

1. He reaps the bearded grain at a breath.
2. Amidst the storm they sang.
3. Choose the timbers with greatest care.
4. A sycamore grew by the door.
5. The clock stood in the corner behind her.
6. I hear the sound of distant footsteps.
7. The key to the drawer is lost.
8. Charity covereth a multitude of sins.
9. They have forgotten the language of their ancestors.
10. They glided calmly down the tranquil stream.

11.   The sad and solemn night
        Hath yet her multitude of cheerful fires.

12. The vine still clings to the mouldering wall.

13. He reads for information.

14. She ran quickly to the spot.

EXERCISE 188

Analyze the following sentences. State clearly the construction of each participial phrase: —

1. The sun having risen, we began our journey.

2. Peace being concluded, I turned my thoughts again to the affairs of the school.

3. Dinner being over, the guests left the room.

4. Looking upward, they beheld the cause of the trouble.

5. Having obtained the information, he ceased questioning.

6. They saw a small vessel, approaching the shore.

7.   All last night we watched the beacons
        Blazing on the hills afar.

8. With every puff of the wind the fire leaped upward from the hearth, laughing and rejoicing at the shrieks of the wintry storm.

9. In the corner of the room stands his gold-headed cane, made of a beautifully polished West India wood.

10. Having lost the confidence of the people, he was compelled to resign his office.

EXERCISE 189

Analyze the following sentences. Be careful to give the construction of each infinitive phrase: —

1. The best course is to confess the fault.

2. It is a noble thing to reward evil with good.

3. It is easy to decide the matter.

4. Strive to be usefully employed.

5. They are about to leave the city.

6. Study to acquire a habit of accurate expression.

7. We should rejoice to hear of the prosperity of others.

8. It is useless to deny the fact.

9. It is very difficult to lay down rules of conduct for others.

10. It would be absurd to make another attempt.

11. The proper business of friendship is to inspire life and courage.

12. One of the hardest things in this world is to see the difference between real dangers and imaginary ones.

13. They were content to consult libraries.

EXERCISE 190

Analyze the following sentences : —

1. The decision of the judge increased the irritation of the people.

2. The best honey is the product of the milder parts of the temperate zone. — JOHN BURROUGHS.

3. The captain's share of the treasure was enough to make him comfortable for the rest of his days. — HAWTHORNE.

4. It is never too late to give up our prejudices.

5. Every man is a missionary for good or for evil.

6. We are equally served by receiving and by imparting.

7. A low, white-washed room, with a stone floor, carefully scrubbed, served for parlor, kitchen, and hall. — IRVING.

8. The turtle, sunning itself upon a rock, slid suddenly into the water with a plunge.

9. It is the glory of a man to pass by an offence.

10. The great secret of a good style is to have proper words in proper places. — E. P. WHIPPLE.

11. A city without mocking-birds is only half Southern.

12. Form the habit of looking for interesting facts in the everyday life about you.

13. How strangely the past is peeping over the shoulders of the present !

14. The words of mercy were upon his lips.

15. Chimney swallows have almost abandoned hollow trees for their nesting-places, even in our most thickly wooded areas, preferring our chimneys.

16. Early next morning I went to visit the grounds.

17. Having been accustomed to the control of large bodies of men, I had not much difficulty in comprehending the situation.

18. Hundreds of other carriages, crowded with their thousands of men, were hastening to the great city.

19. The Stamp Act was a direct tax laid upon the whole American people by Parliament.

20. I see everywhere the gardens, the vineyards, the orchards, with the various greens of the olive, the fig, and the orange.

21. A truly great man borrows no lustre from splendid ancestry.

22. Success being hopeless, preparations were made for a retreat.

23. To bear is to conquer our fate.

CHAPTER LXXXII

THE COMPLEX SENTENCE

A *complex sentence* is a sentence consisting of one principal clause and of one or more subordinate clauses; as, —

He who would search for pearls must dive below.

The principal clause expresses the leading or principal thought of a sentence, but it does not express the complete thought.

The subordinate clause performs the office of a noun, an adjective, or an adverb, and is usually introduced by a conjunction or by a relative pronoun.

I. NOUN CLAUSES

A clause that performs the office of a noun is a *noun clause.* A noun clause may be used —

(1) As the **subject of a verb**; as, —

That you have wronged me doth appear in this.

(2) As a **predicate nominative**; as, —

The result was *that the treaty was signed.*

(3) As the **object of a transitive verb**; as, —

He knows *who wrote the letter.*

(4) As the **logical subject,** defining a foregoing introductory or grammatical subject; as, —

It was a fortunate thing *that we met him.*

(5) As the **object of a preposition**; as, —

The leader encouraged his men by *what he said* and by *what he did.*

Noun clauses are introduced by the conjunctions *that* and *whether*, and by the words *how, when, who, what,* etc.

The conjunction *that* is often omitted when the noun clause follows the principal verb; as, —

I hope [*that*] he will succeed.

EXERCISE 191

In the following sentences, point out the noun clauses used as subjects : —

1. What it cost is of slight importance.
2. "Know thyself" is a comprehensive maxim.
3. What was said was misunderstood.
4. When he will arrive is not yet known.
5. That he should succeed is not surprising.
6. Whoever looks may find the spot.
7. That you have wronged me doth appear in this.
8. How he made his escape is a mystery.
9. What is done cannot be undone.
10. Whoever comes will be welcome.
11. What we achieve depends less on the amount of time we possess, than on the use we make of our time.

EXERCISE 192

In the following sentences, find the noun clauses used as predicate nominatives, and tell to what each refers : —

1. Children are what the mothers are.
2. Be what nature intended you for, and you will succeed.
3. The result was that the troops were defeated.
4. Things are not what they seem.
5. Our hope is that the plan will be accepted.
6. The fact is that he is dissatisfied with the work.

7. The great and decisive test of genius is that it calls forth power in the souls of others.

8. His only chance of escape was that he should go overboard in the night.

In the following sentences, point out the **noun clauses used as objects,** *and tell of what they are objects :* —

1. No man can lose what he never had.
2. I know not what course others may take.
3. What we do not understand, we do not possess.
4. I learned that he was a universal favorite in the village.
5. He declared that he was the sole survivor.
6. See that you can untie what you tie.
7. We do not know how the matter will be decided.
8. I did not understand what was said.
9. His whole mind was occupied by what he had heard.
10. He could describe with great vividness, brevity, and force, what had happened in the past, what actually existed, or what the future promised.
11. No one knows who sent the message.
12. He declared that he was the sole survivor.
13. What we seek, we shall find.
14. Nobody could expect that we should be satisfied with these arrangements.

In the following sentences, point out the **noun clauses used as logical subjects :** —

1. It is good for a man that he bear the yoke in his youth.
2. It has been truly said that he who sets one great truth afloat in the world serves his generation.

3. It is only by degrees that the great body of mankind can be led into new practices.

4. It is seldom that we learn how great a man is until he dies.

5. It was with extreme difficulty that he made his way towards the light.

6. It is not enough to do the right thing, but we must do it in the right way, and at the right time.

7. It is no easy matter to discover the exact spot where a sunken vessel lies.

8. It would be tedious to detail minutely the rest of this story.

II. ADJECTIVE CLAUSES

A clause that performs the office of an adjective is an *adjective clause;* as, —

> Sweet are the thoughts *that savor of content.*
>
> I remember, I remember
> The house *where I was born.*

Adjective clauses are introduced by the relative pronouns *who, which, that,* and by the adverbs *when, where, whence,* etc.

EXERCISE 195

Point out the adjective clauses in the following sentences, and tell what each modifies: —

1. He that is giddy thinks the world turns round.

2. In the evening we reached a village where I had determined to pass the night.

3. It was the time when lilies blow.

4. Here is a barrier that cannot be passed.

5. I had a dream which was not all a dream.

6. He serves all who dares be true.

7. Nature never did betray the heart that loved her.

8. One by one we miss the voices which we loved so well to hear.

III. ADVERBIAL CLAUSES

A clause that performs the office of an adverb is an *adverbial clause.*

An adverbial clause may denote —

(1) **Time,** introduced by *after, before, since, till, when, while;* as, —

> Let us live *while we live.*

(2) **Place,** introduced by *where, whence, whither;* as, —

> I shall remain *where I am.*

(3) **Manner,** introduced by *as;* as, —

> He acts *as no wise man would act.*

(4) **Degree,** introduced by *than, as;* as, —

> My days are swifter *than a weaver's shuttle* [*is*].
> Enough is as good *as a feast* [*is*].

(5) **Cause** or **reason,** introduced by *because, for, since, as, that;* as, —

> Freely we serve, *because we freely love.*
> *Since you desire it,* I will remain.

(6) **Purpose,** introduced by *that, lest;* as, —

> Open the door *that they may enter.*
> Take heed *lest ye fall.*

(7) **Result** or **consequence**, introduced by *so that, that;* as, —

> A storm arose, *so that we could not leave the harbor.*
> What has he done, *that he should be dismissed?*

(8) **Condition**, introduced by *if, unless, except, but;* as, —

> I will go *if you are ready.*
> The house will be sold *unless the money is paid.*
> *Except ye repent,* ye shall all likewise perish.
> It never rains *but it pours.*

(9) **Concession**, introduced by *though, although;* as, —

> *Though he works hard,* he does not succeed.
> *Although he spoke,* he said nothing.

EXERCISE 196

Point out the adverbial clauses of time, and tell what each modifies: —

1. As the last sentence fell from the lips of the reader, a loud shout went up.

2. While she was yet speaking, the sun rose in all its splendor.

3.   She was a phantom of delight
         When first she gleamed upon my sight.

4. When his host had left the room, Dolph remained for some time lost in thought.

5. The sea-birds screamed as they wheeled around.

6. The sun had set before the conflict ended.

7. Write to us as soon as you reach your destination.

8. Fear not, while acting justly.

9. I have not visited the city since you were here.
10. Small service is true service while it lasts.

11.   Days brightly came and calmly went,
           While yet he was our guest.

EXERCISE 197

Point out the **adverbial clauses** *of* **place**, *and tell what each modifies :* —

1. Where your treasure is, there will your heart be also.
2. Whither I go, ye cannot come.
3. Where thoughts kindle, words spontaneously flow.
4. The clouds rolled away to the east, where they lay piled in feathery masses, tinted with the last rosy rays of the sun.
5. Where the heart is well guarded, temptations cannot enter.
6.   Cover the thousands that sleep far away;
           Sleep where their friends cannot find them to-day.

EXERCISE 198

Point out the **adverbial clauses** *of* **manner**, *and tell what each modifies :* —

1. As the tree falls, so it must lie.
2. He died as he lived.
3.   Not as the conqueror comes,
           They, the true-hearted, came.
4. Speak as you think.
5. Forgive us our debts, as we forgive our debtors.
6. We all do fade as a leaf.
7. It droppeth as the gentle rain from heaven.

EXERCISE 199

Find the **adverbial clauses** *of degree, and tell what each modifies :* —

1. Corruption wins not more than honesty.
2. No sooner did this idea enter his head, than it carried conviction with it.
3. The nearer the dawn, the darker the night.
4. The boy ran so fast that I could not overtake him.
5. The result was better than I expected.
6. So far as my own observation goes, the farther one penetrates the sombre solitudes of the woods, the more seldom does one hear the voice of any singing bird.
7. The more time he loses, the poorer he considers himself.
8. The line is so long that it will reach the bottom

EXERCISE 200

Point out the **adverbial clauses** *of cause or reason, and tell how they are joined to the principal clauses :* —

1. We love him because he first loved us.
2. Since they are here, we must receive them.
3. Freely we serve, because we freely love.
4. They deserved respect; for they were good men as well as brave.
5. Since you are acquainted with the facts, you can judge for yourself.
6. As he persisted in refusing help, I left him alone.
7. Our bugles sang truce; for the night-cloud had lowered.
8. As our proposal was rejected, we have nothing further to say.

EXERCISE 201

Point out the adverbial clauses of purpose and of result, and tell what each modifies : —

1. We sow that we may reap.
2. Beware lest you fall.
3. He labored earnestly that abuses might be reformed.
4. I repeated the order that there might be no mistake.
5. Let my people go, that they may serve me.
6. Seek to be so useful, that the world will miss you when away.
7. The day was so still that carts could be heard rumbling a mile away.
8. Love not sleep lest thou come to poverty.

EXERCISE 202

Point out the adverbial clauses of condition, and tell how they are joined to the principal clauses : —

1. Speak clearly if you speak at all ;
   Carve every word before you let it fall.
2. The bill will not become a law, unless the Governor signs it.
3. If he had feared difficulties, he would not have died an acknowledged leader of men.
4. Had you not helped me, I should have failed.
5. If we were base enough to desire it, it is now too late to retire from the contest.
6. If it bear the test, it will be accepted.
7. If I had not been acquainted with the facts, this would have led me into a great error.
8. Had he been absent, the motion would have been carried.
9. This is strange if it be true.
10. If we fail, it can be no worse for us.

EXERCISE 203

*Point out the **adverbial clauses** of **concession,** and tell what each modifies :* —

1. Though it was morning, the sun did not shine.

2. His knowledge, though not always accurate, was of immense extent.

3. The good which men do is not lost, though it is often disregarded.

4. He remained in school, though he was not able to work.

5. Although I had so many interruptions, I completed the work in time.

To the Teacher. — Select, or let the pupils select from their Readers, Histories, or other text-books, many additional sentences containing examples of the different kinds of clauses studied, and require the pupils to point out and classify the clauses and state their construction in the sentence.

IV. ANALYSIS OF COMPLEX SENTENCES

To analyze a complex sentence —

(1) **Tell the kind of sentence.**
(2) **Name the subject and the predicate of the sentence.**
(3) **Tell what the subject consists of.**
(4) **Tell what the predicate consists of.**
(5) **Analyze the subordinate clause or clauses.**

Example I. — That man is formed for social life is acknowledged by all.

Oral Analysis

1. This is a complex declarative sentence.

2. The subject is the noun clause, *that man is formed for social life;* the predicate, *is acknowledged by all.*

3. The predicate consists of the verb *is acknowledged*, modified by the adverbial phrase *by all*.

4. The subordinate clause is introduced by the conjunction *that*.

5. The subject of the subordinate clause is the noun *man*: the predicate, *is formed for social life*.

6. The predicate of the clause consists of the verb *is formed*, modified by the adverbial phrase *for social life*.

WRITTEN ANALYSIS

Complex Declarative Sentence

Complete Subject	That man is formed for social life
Simple Subject	*Noun clause :* that man is formed for social life
Complete Predicate	is acknowledged by all
Simple Predicate	*Verb :* is acknowledged
Modifier	*Adverbial phrase :* by all

Subordinate Clause

Introduced by the conjunction *that*

Subject	*Noun :* man
Complete Predicate	is formed for social life
Simple Predicate	*Verb :* is formed
Modifier	*Adverbial phrase :* for social life

Example II. — The fact that he was present is sufficient.

Oral Analysis

1. This is a complex declarative sentence.
2. The subject is *the fact that he was present;* the predicate, *is sufficient.*
3. The subject consists of the noun *fact,* modified by the adjective *the,* and by the appositive noun clause *that he was present.*
4. The predicate consists of the verb *is,* completed by the adjective *sufficient.*
5. The subordinate clause is introduced by the conjunction *that.*
6. The subject of the subordinate clause is *he;* the predicate, *was present.*
7. The predicate of the clause consists of the verb *was,* completed by the adjective *present.*

Written Analysis

Complex Declarative Sentence

Complete Subject	The fact that he was present
Simple Subject Modifiers	*Noun :* fact *Adjective :* the *Appositive noun clause :* that he was present
Complete Predicate	is sufficient
Simple Predicate Complement	*Verb :* is (*incomplete*) *Adjective :* sufficient

Subordinate Clause

Introduced by the conjunction *that*

Subject	*Pronoun :* he
Complete Predicate	was present
Simple Predicate	*Verb :* was (*incomplete*)
Complement	*Adjective :* present

EXAMPLE III. — The people believed in him, because he was honest and true.

WRITTEN ANALYSIS

Complex Declarative Sentence

Complete Subject	The people
Simple Subject	*Noun :* people
Modifier	*Adjective :* the
Complete Predicate	believed in him, because he was honest and true
Simple Predicate	*Verb :* believed
Modifiers	*Adverbial phrase :* in him *Adverbial clause of reason :* because he was honest and true

Subordinate Clause

Connected to the verb *believed* by the conjunction *because*

Subject	Pronoun : he
Logical Predicate	was honest and true
Gram. Predicate	Verb : was (*incomplete*)
Complement	Adjectives connected by *and* : honest and true

EXERCISE 204

Analyze the sentences in the following exercises : —

1. As we approached the house, we heard the sound of music.

2. Such a fortnight in the woods as I have been lightly sketching, will bring to him who rightly uses it a rich return.

3. If we seek to acquire the style of another, we renounce the individual style which we might have acquired.

4. "Good speed !" cried the watch, as the gate-bolts undrew.

5. So thick were the fluttering snowflakes, that even the trees were hidden by them the greater part of the time.

6. I now found myself among noble avenues of oaks and elms, whose vast size bespoke the growth of centuries.

7. Nothing is so dangerous as pride.

8. We are happy now because God wills it. — LOWELL.

9. A great black cloud had been gathering in the sky for some time past, although it had not yet overspread the sun.

10. Here I sit among my descendants, in my old arm-chair, and immemorial corner, while the firelight throws an appropriate glory round my venerable frame. — HAWTHORNE.

11. He who sets a great example is great. — VICTOR HUGO.

12. I saw from the beach, when the morning was shining,
A bark o'er the waters move gloriously on. — MOORE.

13.   The song that moves a Nation's heart
        Is in itself a deed. — TENNYSON.

14. As I crossed the bridge over the Avon on my return, I paused to contemplate the distant church in which the poet lies buried. — IRVING.

15. We hold these truths to be self-evident : that all men are created equal ; that they are endowed by their Creator with certain unalienable rights ; that among these are life, liberty, and the pursuit of happiness.

16. We can almost fancy that we are visiting him [Milton] in his small lodging ; that we see him sitting at the old organ beneath the faded green hangings ; that we can catch the quick twinkle of his eyes, rolling in vain to find the day ; that we are reading in the lines of his noble countenance the proud and mournful history of his glory and his affliction. — MACAULAY.

17. When the woodpecker is searching for food, or laying siege to some hidden grub, the sound of his hammer is dead or muffled, and is heard but a few yards. It is only upon dry, seasoned timber, freed of its bark, that he beats his reveille to spring and woos his mate. — JOHN BURROUGHS.

18. We are nearer heaven when we listen to the birds than when we quarrel with our fellow-men. — HENRY VAN DYKE.

19.   And the night shall be filled with music,
        And the cares, that infest the day,
        Shall fold their tents, like the Arabs,
        And as silently steal away. — LONGFELLOW.

CHAPTER LXXXIII

THE COMPOUND SENTENCE

A *compound sentence* is a sentence made up of two or more independent members; as, —

> *The walls are high, and the shores are steep.*

Each member of a compound sentence, by itself, forms a complete sentence, which may be simple or complex; as, —

> *The Mayor was dumb* and *the Council stood*
> *As if they were changed into blocks of wood.*

1. The Mayor was dumb.   (Simple sentence.)
2. The Council stood as if they were changed into blocks of wood.   (Complex sentence.)

The connective between the members may be omitted; as, " *The night is chill, the cloud is gray;* " but the relation between the members should be stated in the analysis.

To analyze a compound sentence —

(1) **Tell the kind of sentence.**

(2) **Name the different members, and tell how they are connected.**

(3) **Analyze in order the different members of the sentence.**

EXAMPLE. — The merchants shut up their warehouses, and the laboring men stood idle about the wharves.

ORAL ANALYSIS

1. This is a compound declarative sentence, consisting of two simple members connected by the copulative conjunction *and*.

2. The subject of the first member is *the merchants;* the predicate, *shut up their warehouses.* The subject consists of the noun *merchants*, modified by the adjective *the*. The predicate consists of the verb *shut*, modified by the adverb *up*, and completed by the object *warehouses*. The object is modified by the possessive pronoun *their*.

3. The subject of the second member is *the laboring men;* the predicate, *stood idle about the wharves.* The subject consists of the noun *men*, with the adjectives *the* and *laboring*, of which *laboring* modifies *men*, and *the* modifies *laboring men*. The predicate consists of the verb *stood*, completed by the adjective *idle*, and modified by the adverbial phrase *about the wharves.*

Written Analysis

Compound Declarative Sentence

Two members connected by the conjunction *and*

FIRST MEMBER

Complete Subject	The merchants
Simple Subject	*Noun :* merchants
Modifier	*Adjective :* the
Complete Predicate	shut up their warehouses
Simple Predicate	*Verb :* shut (*incomplete*)
Mod. of Verb	*Adverb :* up
Object	*Noun :* warehouses
Mod. of Object	*Possessive pronoun :* their

SECOND MEMBER

Complete Subject	the laboring men
Simple Subject Modifiers	*Noun :* men *Adjectives :* the, laboring
Complete Predicate	stood idle about the wharves
Simple Predicate Complement Modifier	*Verb :* stood (*incomplete*) *Adjective :* idle *Adverbial phrase :* about the wharves

EXERCISE 205

Analyze the sentences in the following exercises :—

1. Every day is a little life ; and our whole life is but a day repeated.

2. The harvest truly is plenteous, but the laborers are few.

3. They toil not, neither do they spin.

4. It is one thing to be well informed ; it is another to be wise.

5. The ravine was full of sand now, but it had once been full of water.

6. He touched his harp, and nations heard, entranced.

7. The moon is up, and yet it is not night.

8. They had played together in infancy ; they had worked together in manhood ; they were now tottering about, and gossiping away the evening of life ; and in a short time they will probably be buried together in the neighboring churchyard. — IRVING.

9. Now stir the fire, and close the shutters fast.—COWPER.

10.　　Lay down the axe; fling by the spade;
　　　Leave in its track the toiling plough.—BRYANT.

11. But what chiefly characterized the colonists of Merry Mount was their veneration for the Maypole. It has made their true history a poet's tale. Spring decked the hallowed emblem with young blossoms and fresh green boughs; Summer brought roses of the deepest blush, and the perfected foliage of the forest; Autumn enriched it with that red and yellow gorgeousness which converts each wild-wood leaf into a painted flower; and Winter silvered it with sleet, and hung it round with icicles, till it flashed in the cold sunshine, itself a frozen sunbeam.— HAWTHORNE.

CHAPTER LXXXIV

SELECTIONS FOR ANALYSIS

I. THE ARROW AND THE SONG

I shot an arrow into the air,
It fell to earth, I knew not where;
For, so swiftly it flew, the sight
Could not follow it in its flight.

I breathed a song into the air,
It fell to earth, I knew not where;
For who has sight so keen and strong
That it can follow the flight of song?

Long, long afterward, in an oak
I found the arrow, still unbroke;
And the song, from beginning to end,
I found again in the heart of a friend.
　　　　　　　—HENRY WADSWORTH LONGFELLOW.

II. Rip Van Winkle

The great error in Rip's composition was an insuperable aversion to all kinds of profitable labor. It could not be from the want of assiduity or perseverance; for he would sit on a wet rock, with a rod as long and heavy as a Tartar's lance, and fish all day without a murmur, even though he should not be encouraged by a single nibble. He would carry a fowling-piece on his shoulder for hours together, trudging through woods and swamps, and up hill and down dale, to shoot a few squirrels or wild pigeons. He would never refuse to assist a neighbor, even in the roughest toil, and was a foremost man at all country frolics for husking Indian corn or building stone fences. The women of the village, too, used to employ him to run their errands, and to do such little odd jobs as their less obliging husbands would not do for them. In a word, Rip was ready to attend to anybody's business but his own; but as to doing family duty, and keeping his farm in order, he found it impossible.

In fact, he declared it was of no use to work on his farm; it was the most pestilent little piece of ground in the whole country; everything about it went wrong, and would go wrong in spite of him. His fences were continually falling to pieces; his cow would either go astray, or get among the cabbages; weeds were sure to grow quicker in his fields than anywhere else; the rain always made a point of setting in just as he had some outdoor work to do; so that though his patrimonial estate had dwindled away under his management, acre by acre, until there was little more left than a mere patch of Indian corn and potatoes, yet it was the worst-conditioned farm in the neighborhood. — Washington Irving.

III. The Poet's Song

The rain had fallen, the Poet arose,
  He passed by the town and out of the street,
A light wind blew from the gates of the sun,
  And waves of shadow went over the wheat,
And he sat him down in a lonely place,
  And chanted a melody loud and sweet,
That made the wild-swan pause in her cloud,
  And the lark drop down at his feet.

The swallow stopt as he hunted the bee,
  The snake slipt under a spray,
The wild hawk stood with the down on his beak,
  And stared, with his foot on the prey,
And the nightingale thought, " I have sung many songs,
  But never a one so gay,
For he sings of what the world will be
  When the years have died away."— ALFRED TENNYSON.

IV. Leaves

The leaves, as we shall see immediately, are the feeders of the plant. Their own orderly habits of succession must not interfere with their main business of finding food. Where the sun and air are, the leaf must go, whether it be out of order or not. So, therefore, in any group, the first consideration with the young leaves is much like that of young bees, how to keep out of each other's way, that every one may at once leave its neighbors as much free-air pasture as possible, and obtain a relative freedom for itself. This would be a quite simple matter, and produce other simply balanced forms, if each branch, with open air all round it, had nothing to think of but reconcilement of interests among its own leaves. But every branch has others to meet or to cross, sharing with them, in various advantage, what shade, or sun, or rain is to be had. Hence every single leaf-cluster presents the general aspect of a little family, entirely at unity among themselves, but obliged to get their living by various shifts, concessions, and infringements of the family rules, in order not to invade the privileges of other people in their neighborhood. — JOHN RUSKIN.

V. THE CONSTITUTION

What is the Constitution? It is the bond which binds together millions of brothers. What is its history? Who made it? monarchs, crowned heads, lords, or emperors? No, it was none of these. The Constitution of the United States, the nearest approach of mortal to perfect political wisdom, was the work of men who purchased liberty with their blood, but who found that, without organization, freedom was not a blessing. They formed it, and the people, in their intelligence, adopted it. And what has been its history? Has it trodden down any man's rights? Has it circumscribed the liberty of the press? Has it stopped the mouth of any man? Has it held us up as objects of disgrace abroad? How much the reverse! It has given us character abroad; and when, with Washington at its head, it went forth to the world, this young country at once became the most interesting and imposing in the circle of civilized nations. How is the Constitution of the United States regarded abroad? Why, as the last hope of liberty among men. Wherever you go, you find the United States held up as an example by the advocates of freedom. The mariner no more looks to his compass, or takes his departure by the sun, than does the lover of liberty abroad shape his course by reference to the Constitution of the United States. — DANIEL WEBSTER.

PART FIFTH

COMPOSITION

———o◦◦◦◦◦o———

CHAPTER LXXXV

THE PARAGRAPH

I. WHAT A PARAGRAPH IS

Read the following selection, and tell what it is about: —

A Saranac boat is one of the finest things that the skill of man has ever produced under the inspiration of the wilderness. It is a frail shell, so light that a guide can carry it on his shoulders with ease, but so dexterously fashioned that it rides the heaviest waves like a duck, and slips through the water as if by magic. You can travel in it along the shallowest rivers and across the broadest lakes, and make forty or fifty miles a day, if you have a good guide.

— HENRY VAN DYKE, Little Rivers.

A series of sentences relating to a particular point is called a *paragraph*.

A small blank space is usually left at the beginning of the first line in a written or printed paragraph. When a line is begun in this manner, it is said to be **indented**.

EXERCISE 206

State the subject of each of the following paragraphs, and show how each sentence in the paragraph helps in the development of the topic: —

I

The English, from the great prevalence of rural habits throughout every class of society, have always been fond of those festivals and holydays which agreeably interrupt the stillness of country life; and they were in former days particularly observant of the religious and social rites of Christmas. It is inspiring to read even the dry details which some antiquaries have given of the quaint humours, the burlesque pageants, the complete abandonment to mirth and good fellowship, with which this festival was celebrated. It seemed to throw open every door, and unlock every heart. It brought the peasant and the peer together, and blended all ranks in one warm generous flow of joy and kindness. The old halls of castles and manor-houses resounded with the harp and the Christmas carol, and their ample boards groaned under the weight of hospitality. Even the poorest cottage welcomed the festive season with green decorations of bay and holly — the cheerful fire glanced its rays through the lattice, inviting the passenger to raise the latch, and join the gossip knot huddled round the hearth, beguiling the long evening with legendary jokes, and oft-told Christmas tales.

— WASHINGTON IRVING.

II

What are clouds? Is there nothing you are acquainted with which they resemble? You discover at once a likeness between them and the condensed steam of a locomotive. At every puff of the engine a cloud is projected into the air. Watch the cloud sharply; you notice that it first forms at a little distance from the top of the funnel. Give close attention and you will sometimes see a perfectly clear space between the funnel and the cloud. Through that clear space the thing which makes the cloud must pass. What, then, is this thing which at one moment is transparent and invisible, and at the next moment visible as a dense opaque cloud?

It is the *steam* or *vapor of water* from the boiler. Within the boiler this steam is transparent and invisible; but to keep it in this invisible state a heat would be required as great as that within the boiler. When the vapor mingles with the cold air above the hot funnel it ceases to be vapor. Every bit of steam shrinks, when chilled, to a much more minute particle of water. The liquid particles thus produced form a kind of *water-dust* of exceeding fineness, which floats in the air, and is called a *cloud*.

—TYNDALL, Forms of Water.

II. SINGLE PARAGRAPHS

EXERCISE 207

Write a short paragraph about some incident that has taken place in your locality.

Leave a margin half an inch wide at the left of your paper, and a space half an inch long at the beginning of the first line of the paragraph.

Topics for similar exercises:—

1. Effect of last night's frost.
2. A runaway horse.
3. First signs of autumn.
4. A fire.
5. Scene at the railway station.
6. A panic in a school building.
7. A bicycle accident.
8. Condition of our streets.

III. RELATED PARAGRAPHS

THE BUSY BEE

Let us watch the bees as they pass to and fro from their hive. First of all we see some half-dozen around the door. They are there to warn off intruders. If we approach too near the front of the hive, one of these sentries will dash forward with an angry buzz; and, if we do not wisely take the hint, the brave little soldier will soon return with help from the guard-room to enforce the command.

There are three substances required in the hive, — pollen, or bee-bread, the food of the young bees; wax to make the combs; and honey for the support of the community. The bees that are passing and repassing the sentries are not all laden alike. Some of them have little yellow or red tufts on their legs, others have none. But all that return are laden. Those with tufts on their legs have been collecting pollen from flowers. The honey-gatherers and the wax-gatherers carry their stores in their throats.

To understand how the pollen is carried, we should examine a bee's hind leg with a microscope. The upper joint is flattened, and its edges are surrounded with stiff hairs, which form a sort of basket. When the bee enters a flower, it takes a plunge into the pollen. The pollen is brushed down into the little basket, till a good-sized ball is formed. If the bee cannot complete its load in one flower, it will always seek out another of the same kind. It will not mix the pollen of two different kinds of flowers.

The honey-gatherers and the wax-gatherers draw in the sweet juices from flowers by their trunks. The trunk serves as a mouth and a pump. The liquid passes through this into the throat, and is thus carried to the hive.

— Adapted from *Good Words for the Young*.

What do we first see around the door of the hive? What do these bees do? Why are they called *sentries?* What is an *intruder?*

What three substances are required in the hive? What is *pollen?* What is meant by the *community?* What are the bees doing that are passing and repassing the sentries?

Describe a bee's hind leg. How does a bee collect pollen?

How do the honey-gatherers and the wax-gatherers collect their stores?

State the number of paragraphs in this piece, and tell what each is about.

EXERCISE 208

Write from memory what you have learned about the **Bees,** *arranging your statements in four paragraphs. Tell* —

1. What bees are first seen around a hive.

2. What three substances are required in the hive, and the use of each.

3. How a bee collects pollen and carries it to the hive.

4. How the honey-gatherers and the wax-gatherers collect their stores.

CHAPTER LXXXVI

STUDY OF A SELECTION

THE LANDING OF THE PILGRIM FATHERS IN NEW ENGLAND

I

The breaking waves dashed high
On a stern and rock-bound coast,
And the woods against a stormy sky
Their giant branches tossed;

II

And the heavy night hung dark
　　The hills and waters o'er,
When a band of exiles moored their bark
　　On the wild New England shore.

III

Not as the conqueror comes,
　　They, the true-hearted, came;
Not with the roll of the stirring drums,
　　And the trumpet that sings of fame;

IV

Not as the flying come,
　　In silence and in fear; —
They shook the depths of the desert gloom
　　With their hymns of lofty cheer.

V

Amidst the storm they sang,
　　And the stars heard, and the sea;
And the sounding aisles of the dim woods rang
　　To the anthem of the free!

VI

The ocean eagle soared
　　From his nest by the white wave's foam,
And the rocking pines of the forest roared, —
　　This was their welcome home!

VII

There were men with hoary hair
    Amidst that pilgrim band; —
Why had *they* come to wither there,
    Away from their childhood's land?

VIII

There was woman's fearless eye,
    Lit by her deep love's truth;
There was manhood's brow serenely high,
    And the fiery heart of youth.

IX

What sought they thus afar?
    Bright jewels of the mine?
The wealth of seas, the spoils of war?
    They sought a faith's pure shrine!

X

Ay, call it holy ground,
    The soil where first they trod;
They have left unstained what there they found, —
    Freedom to worship God. — FELICIA HEMANS.

What is this poem about? Read the first two stanzas.
What does the first line tell? *Where* did the waves *dash high*?
What is meant by a *stern* coast? What is the meaning of *rock-bound*? What is the meaning of the third and fourth lines?
How would the first two lines in the second stanza be expressed
in prose? On what occasion did the waves *dash high*? What is
an *exile*? What is meant by *mooring their bark*?

Read the next two stanzas. What do the first six lines of these stanzas tell?

Ans. They tell how the exiles did not come.

How many classes of persons are mentioned whose coming was unlike that of the Pilgrims? How does the conqueror come? How do the flying come? What do the two remaining lines of these stanzas tell?

Read the fifth and sixth stanzas. What does the fifth stanza describe? What does the sixth stanza do? What welcomed them?

Read the seventh and eight stanzas. What do these stanzas tell?

Ans. They tell who were in the band.

How many classes of persons are mentioned? Name each. What is the meaning of *hoary?*

Read the first question in the ninth stanza. Supply words making the second question complete. Express the third question fully. What does the last line of this stanza tell? What is meant by their seeking *a faith's pure shrine?*

Ans. Seeking a place where they could worship God in their own way.

Read the last stanza. What place should be called *holy ground?* Why?

EXERCISE 209

Copy the poem, and commit it to memory.

EXERCISE 210

Find out what you can about **The Pilgrim Fathers,** *and then —*

1. Tell in your own words who the Pilgrim Fathers were, and what caused them to leave their native country.

2. Tell where they went first, how long they remained there, and why they decided to come to America.

3. Give an account of their voyage to the New World, tell where they landed, and mention some of the hardships which they had to undergo on their arrival.

CHAPTER LXXXVII

STUDY OF A DESCRIPTION

THE OLD ANGLER'S COTTAGE

I found the old angler living in a small cottage containing only one room, but a perfect curiosity in its method and arrangement.

It was on the skirts of the village, on a green bank, a little back from the road, with a small garden in front, stocked with kitchen herbs, and adorned with a few flowers. The whole front of the cottage was overrun with a honeysuckle. On the top was a ship for a weathercock.

The interior was fitted up in a truly nautical style, the old angler's ideas of comfort and convenience having been acquired on the berth-deck of a man-of-war. A hammock was slung from the ceiling, which, in the daytime, was lashed up so as to take but little room. From the centre of the chamber hung a model of a ship of his own workmanship. Two or three chairs, a table, and a large sea-chest, formed the principal movables. The mantle-piece was decorated with sea-shells; over which hung a quadrant flanked by two woodcuts of most bitter-looking naval commanders. His implements for angling were carefully disposed on nails and hooks about the room. On a shelf was arranged his library, containing a work on angling, much worn, a Bible covered with canvas, an odd volume or two of voyages, a nautical almanac, and a book of songs. — WASHINGTON IRVING.

What is the title of this piece ?   What is an *angler ?*

What does the first sentence tell ?   How many rooms were in the cottage ?   What was a curiosity ?

Where was the cottage ?   What is meant by the *skirts* of the village ?   Where did the cottage stand ?   How far back from the road was it ?   What was in front of the cottage ?   What did the garden contain ?   What is an *herb ?*   Mention two or three kinds of herbs that are commonly raised in gardens.   What else was in the garden ?   What is the meaning of *adorned ?*   Describe the front of the cottage.   What was on the top of it ?   What is a *weathercock ?*

What does the third paragraph describe ?   What is the *interior* of a house ?   What is meant by a *nautical* style ?   What led the old angler to fit up his cottage in the style of a seaman ?   How was his hammock arranged ?   What hung from the centre of the chamber ?   What movable articles of furniture did the room contain ?   What decorated the mantle-piece ?   What hung over it ?   What is a *quadrant ?*   What is meant by the quadrant's being *flanked* by the two woodcuts ?   What hung on the nails and hooks about the room ?   Where was the library ?   Of what books was it composed ?

EXERCISE 211

REPRODUCTION

THE OLD ANGLER'S COTTAGE

*Write in your own words a description of **The Old Angler's Cottage**.*

EXERCISE 212

DESCRIPTION OF A ROOM

Write a description of some room that you have seen.   Tell what things were in the room, and how they were arranged.

Topics for similar descriptions : —

1. A village store.
2. Our schoolroom.
3. A blacksmith shop.

4. A country church.
5. A family sitting-room.
6. A fire station.

CHAPTER LXXXVIII

ORAL COMPOSITION

The Nest of the Bobolink

Read the following selections : —

I

If I were a bird, in building my nest I should follow the example of the bobolink, placing it in the midst of a broad meadow, where there was no spear of grass, or flower, or growth unlike another to mark its site. I judge that the bobolink escapes the dangers to which I have adverted as few or no other birds do. Unless the mowers come along at an earlier date than she has anticipated, that is, before July 1, or a skunk goes nosing through the grass, which is unusual, she is as safe as bird well can be in the great open of nature. She selects the most monotonous and uniform place she can find amid the daisies or the timothy and clover, and places her simple structure upon the ground in the midst of it. There is no concealment, except as the great conceals the little, as the desert conceals the pebble, as the myriad conceals the unit. You may find the nest once, if your course chances to lead you across it and your eye is quick enough to note the silent brown bird as she darts quickly away ; but step three paces in the wrong direction, and your search will probably be fruitless. — John Burroughs.

II

The bobolinks build in considerable numbers in a meadow within a quarter of a mile of us. A houseless lane passes through the midst of their camp, and in clear westerly weather, at the right season, one may hear a score of them singing at once. When they are breeding, if I chance to pass, one of the male birds always accompanies me like a constable, flitting from post to post of the rail-fence, with a short note of reproof continually repeated, till I am fairly out of the neighborhood. Then he will swing away into the air and run down the wind, gurgling music without stint over the unheeding tussocks of meadow-grass and dark clumps of bulrushes that mark his domain. — JAMES RUSSELL LOWELL.

EXERCISE 213

Tell in your own words where the bobolink builds its nest, why the situation chosen is a safe one, and how the male bird strives to conceal from the passer-by the location of the nest.

CHAPTER LXXXIX

EXERCISES IN NARRATION AND DESCRIPTION

EXERCISE 214

NESTING OF A FAMILIAR BIRD

Write an account of some bird that nests in your locality.

1. Tell whether the bird is a permanent or a summer resident, and if the latter, at what time it arrives in the spring.

2. State the date of nesting, and give particulars about the situation and the construction of the nest.

3. State the number of eggs in a set, and tell how many broods are raised in a season.

4. Add any facts that interest you about these birds.

EXERCISE 215

MIGRATION OF BIRDS

Find out what you can about the **Migration of Birds,** *and then —*

1. Tell what the migration of a bird is.

2. Name the common migratory birds in your locality, and tell at what time they arrive in spring, and when they depart in autumn.

3. Tell why these birds migrate. State whether they feed upon insects, worms, fruit, seeds, fish, or other food, and show what effect the cold weather has upon their supply of food.

4. Tell how they migrate, — whether they travel in the daytime or at night, alone or in flocks, — and where they go.

EXERCISE 216

Compare any two of the following, and state clearly some of the most striking points of resemblance and difference in their structure, habits, or uses : —

Butterflies and Moths,	Crabs and Lobsters,
Toads and Frogs,	Alligators and Crocodiles,
Snakes and Eels,	Rabbits and Hares,
Clams and Oysters,	Goats and Sheep.

Model. — BUTTERFLIES AND MOTHS

Butterflies and moths when flying look very much alike. Butterflies, however, fly only in the daytime, while most moths fly at night.

Butterflies as well as moths have four wings. When a butterfly is at rest, it holds its wings erect. When a moth is at rest, its wings are folded over the body like a flat roof.

EXERCISE 217

Write about some article that is prepared for market near your home; as, —

coal	tobacco	wheat	granite
cotton	petroleum	butter	maple sugar

State, so far as you know, the different steps taken in the process of cultivation or manufacture, and tell in what form and in what way the article is taken to market.

CHAPTER XC

STUDY OF A DESCRIPTION

THE SNOW-STORM

(*From "Snow-Bound"*)

The sun that brief December day
Rose cheerless over hills of gray,
And, darkly circled, gave at noon
A sadder light than waning moon.
Slow tracing down the thickening sky
Its mute and ominous prophecy,
A portent seeming less than threat,
It sank from sight before it set.

A chill no coat, however stout,
Of homespun stuff could quite shut out,
A hard, dull bitterness of cold,
    That checked, mid-vein, the circling race
    Of life-blood in the sharpened face,
The coming of the snow-storm told.
The wind blew east; we heard the roar
Of Ocean on his wintry shore,
And felt the strong pulse throbbing there
Beat with low rhythm our inland air.

     *   *   *   *   *

Unwarmed by any sunset light
The gray day darkened into night,
A night made hoary with the swarm
And whirl-dance of the blinding storm,
As zigzag wavering to and fro
Crossed and recrossed the wingéd snow:
And ere the early bedtime came
The white drift piled the window-frame,
And through the glass the clothes-line posts
Looked in like tall and sheeted ghosts.

So all night long the storm roared on:
The morning broke without a sun;
In tiny spherule traced with lines
Of Nature's geometric signs,
In starry flake, and pellicle,
All day the hoary meteor fell;
And, when the second morning shone,
We looked upon a world unknown,
On nothing we could call our own.

Around the glistening wonder bent
The blue walls of the firmament,
No cloud above, no earth below, —
A universe of sky and snow!
The old familiar sights of ours
Took marvellous shapes; strange domes and towers
Rose up where sty or corn-crib stood,
Or garden wall, or belt of wood;
A smooth white mound the brush-pile showed,
A fenceless drift what once was road;
The bridle-post an old man sat
With loose-flung coat and high cocked hat;
The well-curb had a Chinese roof;
And even the long sweep, high aloof,
In its slant splendor, seemed to tell
Of Pisa's leaning miracle.[1] — JOHN GREENLEAF WHITTIER.

What statement is made in the first two lines? Where was the cheerless sun seen? When? What word describes the appearance of the hills?

To what is the light of the sun compared in the second statement? Why *waning* moon? What words in the third line describe the appearance of the sun at noon?

What is the third fact stated about the sun? What is meant by the thickening sky? What is the sun called in the seventh line? What is a *portent?* Tell what signs of the coming snow-storm are mentioned in the first eight lines.

Read the next ten lines. What is the first thing mentioned in these lines that indicated the approaching snow-storm? What shows the degree of the chill? Why would a coat of "homespun stuff" be

[1] This line refers to the Leaning Tower of Pisa.

more likely to shut out the chill than any other coat? What was the effect of the chill upon the face? Why? How did the wind indicate the coming of the storm? What is meant by the *throbbing pulse* of the ocean?

Read the next ten lines. When did it begin snowing? What is the meaning of *hoary?* To what does the use of the word *swarm* direct the attention? The word *whirl-dance?* What showed the depth of the snow at early bedtime?

Read the next nine lines. How long did the storm continue? Read the part in these lines descriptive of the snow-flakes. What is the meaning of *pellicle?* What does the use of the word *shone* imply about the state of the weather on the second morning?

Read the remaining lines. What is meant by the *glistening wonder?* What is the meaning of the line, *No cloud above, no earth below?* What is said about the old familiar sights? What did the sty or corn-crib resemble? The brush-pile? The road? The bridle-post? The well-curb? The well-sweep?

How does this description of a snow-storm accord with your own observations?

EXERCISE 218

Study carefully the foregoing description of a snow-storm, and then tell in your own words —

1. How the sun, the chill, the wind, and the ocean indicated the coming of the snow-storm.

2. At what time it began to snow, and how long the storm continued.

3. What was seen on the second morning.

CHAPTER XCI

LETTER–WRITING

I. THE PARTS OF A LETTER

A letter is made up of five parts. (See Form on next page.)

If a letter fills a page or more, it should begin about an inch and a half from the top of the page. But if it occupies only a few lines, it should begin lower down, so that the margins above and below the letter may be about equal. The first line of the heading should begin a little to the left of the middle of the page.

A margin should be left on the left-hand side of each page. The width of this margin should be about one-quarter of an inch on note-paper, and about half an inch on large letter-paper.

The address is usually placed at the beginning of a business letter and at the close of a familiar letter.

When the address is placed at the close of a letter, the salutation should begin at the marginal line, on the first line below the heading, and the body of the letter should begin at the end of the salutation, on the first line below.

EXERCISE 219

(1) *Copy on note-paper the following letter-form. Leave on the left-hand side of the page a margin one-quarter of an inch wide, and arrange the different parts as they are arranged in the model given.*

[HEADING.]

Santa Barbara, Cal.,

Dec. 6, 1899.

[SALUTATION.]

My dear Brother, –

[BODY OF LETTER.]

[CONCLUSION.]

Your loving sister,

Grace E. Holmes.

[ADDRESS.]

Mr. Frank S. Holmes,

Madison, Wis.

(2) *Write a letter-form similar to the one given on page 277, using in it your own name and address, and the name and address of one of your friends. Draw dotted lines to represent the body of the letter.*

II. THE HEADING

The **heading** of a letter shows where the letter was written and when it was written.

If the letter is written from a city, the heading should contain the number of the house, the name of the street, the name of the city, and the name of the state.

NOTE. — Sometimes the number of the post-office box is used instead of the number of the house and the name of the street.

If the letter is written from a small town, the heading should contain not only the name of the town and the name of the state, but the name of the county also.

If the letter is written from a large school, from a hotel, or from any well-known institution, the name of the institution may take the place of the street and number.

The heading should begin about an inch and a half from the top of the page, and a little to the left of the middle. If the heading is short, it may be written on one line. If it occupies two or three lines, the second line should begin a little farther to the right than the first, and the third line should begin a little farther to the right than the second.

Name the different items in each heading. What mark is used to separate these parts? What mark is placed at the close of each heading?

FORMS OF HEADING

1

Rutland, Vermont, May 8, 1899.

2

Lenox, Berkshire Co., Mass.,
March 2, 1900.

3

116 Martin St., Milwaukee, Wis.,
Feb. 22, 1899.

4

P. O. Box 725, Denver, Col.,
Sept. 25, 1900.

5

Vassar College,
Poughkeepsie, N. Y.,
Dec. 13, 1899.

Separate by commas the different items in the heading, and place a period at the close of the heading.

NOTE. — If any of the words in the heading of a letter are abbreviated, the different items must be separated by commas, just as if the words were written in full. A period must be placed after each abbreviation.

Do not omit the name of the state from the heading of a letter; thus, not *Springfield, July* 24, 1902.

Do not abbreviate the name of a city; not *N. Y.* for *New York*.

Do not abbreviate the distinguishing word in the name of a county; thus, not *Scho. Co.* for *Schoharie Co.*, *Wash. Co.* for *Washington Co.*

Do not write *st*, *d*, or *th* after the number denoting the day of the month, when that number is immediately followed by the number denoting the year; not *Jan*. 1st, 1905, for *Jan*. 1, 1905; *May* 3d, 1901, for *May* 3, 1901; *Dec*. 25th, 1906, for *Dec*. 25, 1906.

EXERCISE 220

Copy the foregoing headings. Be careful to arrange the different parts as they are arranged in the forms given.

EXERCISE 221

Write headings for letters from the items given below. Arrange the items like those in the foregoing forms.

1. Austin, Texas, May 3, 1903.

2. 839 Wabash Avenue, Chicago, Illinois, November 15, 1900.

3. Cooperstown, Otsego County, New York, August 26, 1902.

4. Yale College, New Haven, Connecticut, February 22, 1901.

5. Philadelphia, Pennsylvania, January 17, 1899. P.O. Box 947.

EXERCISE 222

Write a heading for a letter to be sent from your home to-day.

III. THE SALUTATION

The **salutation** consists of the opening words of respect or affection.

FORMS OF SALUTATION

To relatives or friends —

Dear Father, —   My dear Clara, —
My dear Mother, —   Dear Uncle Henry, —
My dear Sister, —   Dear Miss Edwards, —
Dear Edward : —   Dear Mr Harper : —

To others —

Madam : —   Dear Madam : —
Sir : —   Dear Sir : —
Dear Sirs : —   Gentlemen : —

NOTE. — Some writers make a distinction in the use of the terms of address "Dear Sirs" and "Gentlemen," using the former term in letters purely commercial, and the latter term in addressing firms of lawyers, boards of education, officers of an institution, or others acting in their official capacity.

When the words *father*, *mother*, *sister*, *cousin*, etc., are used in the salutation of a letter, they should begin with capital letters.

The salutation may be followed by a comma and a dash, or by a colon and a dash.

NOTE. — Some writers do not use the dash in the salutation unless the body of the letter begins on the same line as the salutation.

When the address is placed at the close of a letter, the salutation should begin at the marginal line, on the first line below the heading; but when the address is placed at the beginning of a letter, the salutation should be placed on the first line below the address. (See p. 277, and pp. 285 and 286, Ex. 1 and 2.)

EXERCISE 223

Copy the foregoing forms of salutation.

EXERCISE 224

Write a salutation for a letter to —

     1. Your mother or your guardian.
     2. A lady who is a stranger.
     3. A gentleman who is a stranger.
     4. A business firm.

5. Your teacher.   7. One of your classmates.
6. Your aunt.   8. Your cousin.

IV. THE CONCLUSION

The **conclusion** of a letter is made up of the closing words of respect or affection and the signature of the writer.

Forms of Conclusion

1

---------------------------------.

Lovingly yours,
Alice L. Martin.

2

-------------------------------------.

Most sincerely yours,
George H. Reynolds.

3

-----------------------------------.

Your loving daughter,
Fanny S. Austin

4

----- ---------------.

Respectfully yours,
Charles R. Thompson.

With what kind of letter does each conclusion begin? What mark separates the closing words from the name of the writer? What mark is placed after the signature?

The first word of the conclusion should begin with a capital letter.

The closing words should be separated from the signature of the writer by a comma.

A period should be placed after the signature of the writer.

Some of the forms used in closing familiar letters are: —

Your loving son.	Your affectionate father.
Lovingly yours.	Faithfully yours.
Affectionately yours.	Cordially yours.
Sincerely yours.	Very sincerely yours.

The most common forms for closing business letters are: —

Yours respectfully.	Yours truly.
Respectfully yours.	Very truly yours.

When the words, *sister*, *brother*, *friend*, etc., are used in the conclusion of a letter, they should begin with small letters. (See Form 3, p. 283.)

EXERCISE 225

Copy the foregoing forms of conclusion.

EXERCISE 226

(1) *Write five different forms for closing familiar letters.*
(2) *Write five different forms for closing business letters.*

V. THE ADDRESS

The **address** is made up of the name, the title, and the residence or place of business of the person written to.

NOTE. — If the letter is an important one, the address should contain not only the name of the place where the letter is to be sent, but the street and number, the county, or such other items as make up the full address. But in ordinary letters the name of the city or town and the name of the state will be sufficient. Many persons omit the address altogether in familiar letters.

In business letters, the address of the person written to is usually placed at the beginning of the letter; but in other letters it is written at the close of the letter. When the address is placed at the beginning of a letter, it should begin at the marginal line, on the first line below the heading (see Business Letter p. 292); but when it is placed at the close of a letter, it should begin at the marginal line, on the first line below the signature (see p. 277).

FORMS OF ADDRESS

1. — Business Letter

Rev. John S. Howard,
     Portland, Me.
               Dear Sir:– Your favor
of Feb. 27th, requesting us, etc.

2. — Business Letter

Messrs. W. H. Sellars & Co.,
913 Broadway,
Indianapolis, Ind.
Dear Sirs:— In reply to
yours of the 28th inst., etc.

3. — Familiar Letter

-----------------------------------.

Your loving daughter,
Edith L. Brown.
Dr. Lansing N. Brown,
Ann Arbor, Mich.

Name the different items in each address and tell how those parts are separated. What mark is placed at the close of each address?

Separate the different parts of the address by commas, and place a period at its close.

Do not forget to use a title when writing a person's address. Some of the most common titles used in addresses are:

I.— BEFORE THE NAMES OF PERSONS

Mrs.[1]	Miss	Mr.	Rev.	Prof.
Master	Misses	Messrs.	Dr.	Hon.

Prefix *Mrs.* to the name of a married woman; *Miss* to the name of an unmarried woman; *Mr.* to the name of a man who has no higher title; and *Master* to the name of a boy. In writing to two or more gentlemen, use the title *Messrs.;* to two or more young ladies, the title *Misses*. Prefix *Rev.* to the name of a clergyman, or *Rev. Mr.* if the Christian name is not known; *Dr.* to the name of a physician; *Prof.* to the name of one who has been elected to a professorship in a college or other institution of learning; and *Hon.* to the name of a cabinet officer, a member of Congress, a judge, a mayor, and to the names of some others of similar rank.

NOTE. — When a lady writes to a stranger, she should prefix *Miss* or *Mrs.*, in parentheses, to her name, so that the person who answers the letter may know how to address the reply.

II.— AFTER THE NAMES OF PERSONS

Esq.[1]   A.M.   M.D.   Ph.D.   D.D.   LL.D.

Esq. is added to the name of a member of the legal profession, and to the names of civil officers not entitled to the prefix *Hon.* *A.M.*, *M.D.*, *Ph.D.*, *D.D.*, and *LL.D.* are titles conferred by universities, colleges, or other institutions of learning.

Do not prefix *Mr.* to a name when *Esq.*, *A.M.*, or some similar title is added to the name; and do not prefix *Dr.* to a

[1] The meanings of these titles are given in the list of abbreviations on pages 319–321.

name that is followed by one of the titles, *M.D.*, *Ph.D.*, *D.D.*, or *LL.D.;* thus, not *Dr. John Brown, M.D.*, but *Dr. John Brown*, or *John Brown, M.D.* Not *Rev. Dr. Henry S. White, D.D.*, but *Rev. Dr. Henry S. White*, or *Rev. Henry S. White, D.D.*

EXERCISE 227

Write addresses to be used in letters to —

A married lady.	A boy.	A clergyman.
An unmarried lady.	An editor.	A physician.
A member of Congress.	A business firm.	A lawyer.

VI. THE BODY OF A LETTER

The **body of a letter** usually begins at the end of the salutation, on the first line below it (see p. 277); but when the address and salutation together occupy more than two lines, the body of the letter is often begun on the same line with the salutation. (See pp. 286 and 292.)

Adapt the style of the letter to the subject. In writing to relatives or to intimate friends, be unreserved — write as you would talk if your friends were present. In writing to superiors or to strangers, be respectful.

Begin at once with what you wish to say, and when you have finished do not try to think of something to fill the sheet, but add the closing words of respect or affection, and sign your name.

Do not write a succession of short sentences with the subjects omitted; as, *Had a pleasant journey. Found my friends well. Shall expect to hear from you soon.*

Do not begin a new paragraph under the last word of the preceding paragraph, but leave a space the width of the margin at the beginning of the first line in every paragraph, except the first.

Do not rule a line for the margin of a letter.

When you use the letters *st*, *d*, or *th* after the day of the month, do not write them above the line, but on the line; as, Dec. 16*th*, not Dec. 16$\frac{th}{\pi}$.

Do not place periods after 1*st*, 2*d*, 3*d*, 4*th*, etc.

Do not place two periods at the close of a sentence when the last word is abbreviated.

Do not send a letter carelessly written. Pay particular attention to penmanship, capital letters, and marks of punctuation.

If writing to a person who is not a near relative or a close friend, do not forget to enclose a postage stamp when you write requesting an answer for your own benefit.

EXERCISE 228

Write a letter to one of your cousins or to some other friend, describing your school. Tell the number of pupils, the number of teachers, and such other things about the school as interest you most.

Follow the form given on page 277. Give your full address in the heading, and sign your own name to the letter.

EXERCISE 229

Suppose that you are away from home attending school. Write a letter to some member of your family, requesting to have some article that you need sent to you.

VII. THE SUPERSCRIPTION

The address on the envelope is called the **superscription**.

FORMS OF SUPERSCRIPTION

STAMP

Miss Elizabeth S. Howard,
95 Front Street,
Binghamton,
New York.

STAMP

Rev. Henry M. Porter, D. D.,
Norwalk,
P. O. Box 317.
Conn.

Write the first line of the address near the middle of the envelope, making the right and left margins equal. Begin each of the other lines a little farther to the right than the preceding line.

Notice that in the forms of superscription given the different items are separated by commas, and the last item is followed by the period. Many persons use no marks of punctuation in the superscription, except the period after an abbreviation.

Place the stamp at the upper right-hand corner of the envelope.

To fold a sheet of ordinary note-paper so that it will fit an envelope a little longer than the width of the sheet, lay the sheet before you with the first page up, and the double edge toward your left hand. Then turn the lower third of the sheet up, fold the upper third down over this, and press the folds.

If a large square envelope is used, only one fold should be made. Place the sheet before you in the manner described, turn the lower part of the sheet up until the lower and upper edges meet, and press the fold.

EXERCISE 230

(1) *Copy on envelopes the foregoing superscriptions.*

(2) *Write on envelopes the superscriptions of letters to be sent to —*

1. Your father or guardian.   3. Your teacher.
2. One of your classmates.   4. A business firm.
5. Your uncle in a distant city.

VIII. A BUSINESS LETTER

FORM OF BUSINESS LETTER

Hartford, Conn., Sept. 7, 1905.
Messrs. D. C. Heath & Co.,
110 Boylston Street,
Boston, Mass.

Dear Sirs:— Enclosed is an order for three dollars and ninety-five cents ($3 $\frac{95}{100}$), for which please send me, by express, the following books:—

6 The Sir Roger de Coverley Papers.
1 Carlyle's Essay on Burns.
2 George Eliot's Silas Marner.
2 Scott's Ivanhoe.
1 Webster's First Bunker Hill Oration.

Yours truly,
Edward Sherman.

NOTE.— If you are ordering books that are published in various styles, state in your order not only the title of the book, but also the edition and style of binding that you prefer. It is well to state also the author's name.

EXERCISE 231

Copy the foregoing letter. Pay particular attention to capital letters, marks of punctuation, and the arrangement of the different parts.

EXERCISE 232

Write to the publishers of your Reader or your Geography, and order a sufficient number of copies of the book to supply your class.

IX. LETTERS ORDERING PERIODICALS

EXERCISE 233

Write a letter ordering " St. Nicholas," " Youth's Companion," or some other magazine or paper that you would like to take. Use your own name and address in the letter.

X. ORDERS

EXERCISE 234

Write to William Gray, Canton, N.Y., ordering the following seeds to be sent, by mail, to your address : —

1 pkg. Pansy, light blue, 15 cts.; 1 pkg. Pansy, King of the Blacks, 15 cts.; 1 pkg. Verbena, scarlet, 20 cts.; 1 pkg. Verbena, mixed varieties, 20 cts.; 1 pkg. Sweet Mignonette, 5 cts.; 1 oz. Sweet Peas, mixed colors, 10 cts.

EXERCISE 235

Write a letter to some business firm that you know, ordering goods of some kind. State clearly the number and kind of articles that you desire, and tell how you wish them sent.

XI. APPLICATION FOR A POSITION

Beloit, Wis., June 1, 1901.

To the Board of Education,
      Madison, Wis.

Gentlemen : —

Learning that there is to be a vacancy in Grammar School No. 2 of your city, I write to make application for the position.

I graduated at the Orient Normal School in 1898, and have been teaching since that time.

Enclosed you will find testimonials from the President of the institution from which I graduated and from the Superintendent of Schools where I have been teaching.

Should a personal interview be desired, I shall be glad to present myself at such time and place as you may name.

Very respectfully yours,

(Miss) Agnes Marshall.

EXERCISE 236

Copy the foregoing letter. Pay particular attention to the use of capital letters and marks of punctuation, and to the arrangement of the different parts.

EXERCISE 237

Write to the Board of Education in some city in your State, making application for a position as teacher in one of the public schools of that city.

XII.   LETTER OF INTRODUCTION

Anderson, Ind., Jan. 4, 1902.

Dear Mrs. Chapman,—

This letter will introduce to you my friend, Miss Mabel Howard, who is spending the winter in New York for the purpose of studying music. Any attention that you may be able to show her will be warmly appreciated by

Your sincere friend,

Emma Gilbert.

Mrs. John Chapman,
848 Fifth Avenue, New York.

 EXERCISE 238

Write a letter introducing a young friend of yours to one of your former teachers who lives in a distant city.

XIII.   REQUEST FOR A CATALOGUE

Williamsport, Ind., July 17, 1903.

The Registrar,
American University,
Washington, D. C.

Dear Sir:—

Please send me a catalogue of the American University, and greatly oblige,

Yours respectfully,

Albert Raymond.

Write to a publisher of books, and ask him to send you a catalogue of his publications.

CHAPTER XCII

BUSINESS FORMS

I. BILLS

1

Chicago, Nov. 1, 1904.

Mr. Lyman Gilbert,

Bought of Smith & Howard.

50 lbs. Coffee Sugar,	. . .	@	8¢	$ 4	00
10 lbs. Java Coffee,	. . .	"	35¢	3	50
4 lbs. Oat Meal,	. . .	"	5¢		20
8 doz. Eggs,	. . .	"	20¢	1	60
4 gals. Molasses,	. . .	"	70¢	2	80
50 lbs. Butter,	. . .	"	25¢	12	50
2 doz. Lemons,	. . .	"	15¢		30
				24	90

Received Payment,

Smith & Howard,
per Scott.

When a bill is paid, the person to whom the money was due gives a receipt, or writes "Received Payment," and signs his name. The latter is called *receipting a bill*.

When a clerk receipts a bill, he signs the name of his employer, and then writes his own name below, after the Latin word *per* = by. In the foregoing example, a clerk named *Scott* receipted the bill for his employers.

What should be written first in a bill? Where should the name of the person that buys the articles be written? Where should the name of the person or firm that sells the articles be written? How are the names of the articles written?

2

Philadelphia, April 23, 1900.

Miss Helen R. White,

To Margaret D. Harris, Dr.

1900				$	
Mar.	3	1	Mozart Sonata	$	50
"	9	1	Haydn Sonata		75
"	19	1	Nocturno, Zimmermann		50
Apr.	3	1	Songs without Words, Mendelssohn .	1	00
"	9	1	Rondo, Beethoven		35
"	23	1	Term Instruction	20	00
				$23	10

Received Payment,

Margaret D. Harris.

Of what is the second bill a record? Where are the different items placed? Where are the dates written? What words should not be written until the bill is paid?

EXERCISE 240

Rule paper as in the models given, and copy the two bills.

EXERCISE 241

Herman Fuller bought the following articles of Bell and Norton, Minneapolis, Minn., Dec. 17, 1900 : 1 Saddle @ $15 ; 1 Bridle @ $5 ; 1 Riding Whip @ $2 ; 2 pairs Skates @ $2.50 ; 2 Pocket Knives @ 75¢ ; 1 Hatchet @ $1.25.

Make out the bill, and receipt it in the name of the firm.

EXERCISE 242

Mrs. Harriet West of Buffalo, N.Y., made a dress for Mrs. Orlando Foster. She furnished the following articles : 8 yds. Percaline @ 25¢ ; 4 yds. Binding @ 6¢ ; 1 doz. Buttons @ $1.00 ; 3 Whalebones @ 25¢ ; Braid, Silk, and Twist, 40¢. She charged $10 for making the dress.

Make out a receipted bill, dated to-day. Follow the Form given on page 296.

II. RECEIPTS

A written acknowledgment of money or goods received is called a **receipt** ; as, —

1

$60.$\frac{12}{00}$.   Baltimore, Md., Mar. 1, 1899.

Received from George S. Abbott Sixty and $\frac{12}{00}$ Dollars, to balance account.

M. J. Blair.

2

$ 30 $\frac{00}{100}$.   Chicago, June 1, 1900.

Received from Helen M. Crawford
Thirty Dollars, for board to this date.

Mrs. C. K. Wright.

When is a receipt given?   By whom is it signed?   In how many places is the amount written?   How is it written?   Why is it written twice?

For what purpose was the first sum paid?   What is meant by "balancing" an account?

EXERCISE 243

Copy the foregoing receipts. Be careful to arrange the different parts like those in the models given.

EXERCISE 244

Suppose Walter D. Moore rents a house that you own. On the first day of this month he paid you thirty dollars for rent of house to that time.

Write a receipt for the amount received. Follow the Form given above.

EXERCISE 245

Look at the bills on pages 296 and 297 and write the two receipts that might have been given in place of the receipted bills.

III. ADVERTISEMENTS FOR ARTICLES LOST

LOST. — On Saturday afternoon, between the Commercial Bank and the Post Office, a small black morocco pocket-book, containing a check on the Commercial Bank and one or two dollars in silver.   The finder will be suitably rewarded upon leaving the article at 714 Broadway.

What was lost?   What does the phrase *on Saturday afternoon* tell?   What does the second phrase tell?   What words describe the pocket-book?   What did the pocket-book contain?   Where was the finder requested to leave the article?

When you write an advertisement about an article that is lost, describe the article so clearly that it may be known from your description.

EXERCISE 246

You have lost one of the articles named below.   Write an advertisement about the lost article, to be inserted in one of the papers in your town.

bracelet   knife   dog   horse

IV. ADVERTISEMENTS FOR ARTICLES FOUND

FOUND. — On Main Street, last Friday morning, a watch. The owner can have the article by calling at this office, proving the property, and paying for this notice.

What article was found?   Where was it found?   When was it found?   What is meant by *proving the property?*

When you write an advertisement about an article that has been found, do *not* describe the article fully, lest the wrong person should claim it.

EXERCISE 247

You have found one of the things named below. Write a notice for a paper, advertising the article.

muff   coat   bank-book   travelling-bag

V. ADVERTISEMENTS FOR HELP

1

WANTED. — A neat, strong girl for general housework; must understand cooking; references required. Apply at 189 West 57th Street.

2

WANTED. — A bright, active, honest boy for office-work. Apply by letter, stating age and giving references. Address Dr. L. B. Porter, P. O. Box 1247, New York.

What is the first advertisement for? What qualifications must the girl have? How is the applicant expected to apply?

What is the second advertisement for? How is the applicant to apply?

EXERCISE 248

(1) *Copy the foregoing advertisements.*

(2) *Write an advertisement asking for a woman or a girl to take care of young children. Mention some of the qualities that the applicant must possess.*

(3) *Write a letter in answer to the second advertisement above. Give for reference the name of your teacher.*

NOTE. — Do not forget the proper form for the heading, the address, and the other parts. Remember that a neat, well-written letter, sent in answer to an advertisement, will aid the applicant in securing the desired position.

VI. ADVERTISEMENTS FOR SITUATIONS

WANTED. — By a young man, a situation as coachman; understands the care of horses and is a careful driver; good references. Address F. B., 325 Third Avenue.

Who advertises for a situation? What situation does he wish? What does the writer say he can do?

EXERCISE 249

(1) *Write an advertisement for a situation as gardener.*
(2) *Write an advertisement for a situation as cook.*
(3) *Write an advertisement for a situation as janitor.*
(4) *A dressmaker wishes to go out by the day. Write an advertisement for her.*

VII. NOTICES OF PUBLIC MEETINGS

The annual meeting of the Woman's Foreign Missionary Society will be held at the Fourth Presbyterian Church on Tuesday, the 25th inst., at 3 o'clock P.M.

Of what meeting is this a notice? Where is it to be held? When is it to be held?

EXERCISE 250

Rev. William Howard, D.D., will deliver a lecture on Temperance at some church or hall in your place. Write a notice of the lecture.

EXERCISE 251

Some society in your place is to hold an annual meeting for the election of officers. Write a notice of the meeting.

EXERCISE 252

Your school is to have public exercises. Write a notice telling where and when the exercises are to be held.

EXERCISE 253

Write public notices similar to those you heard read from the pulpit last Sunday.

VIII. TELEGRAPHIC DESPATCHES

EXERCISE 254

Write, from the items given below, telegraphic despatches of not more than ten words each.

The address and the signature are not to be counted as part of the ten words.

1

Hanover, N.H., Dec. 17, 1901.

Mrs. G. W. Hall,
     Rutland, Vt.

I shall not reach home to-night, on account of a railroad accident. No one is injured.   G. W. Hall.

2

Ithaca, N.Y., March 18, 1907.

Mr. H. R. Baker,
     Omaha, Neb.

The house is sold, and possession is to be given on May 1st. I have written you full particulars.
                                R. S. Allen.

3

Baltimore, Md., Dec. 18, 1004.

To the Passenger Agent of the
    Delaware, Lackawanna, and Western Railroad,
      285 Broadway, New York.

Please reserve for me a lower berth in the sleeping-car
that leaves New York for Oswego on Friday, the 23d inst.

                    S. T. Norton.

CHAPTER XCIII

SOCIAL FORMS

FORMAL INVITATIONS

Formal invitations are expressed in the third person : thus—

Mr. and Mrs. Edward Stanley

request the pleasure of

Mr. William King's

company at dinner

on Tuesday, June nineteenth,

at seven o'clock.

927 Oak Avenue.

The note of acceptance or regret should correspond in form to the invitation, as in the following examples:—

Mr. William King
accepts with pleasure
Mr. and Mrs. Edward Stanley's
kind invitation
for Tuesday, June nineteenth,
at seven o'clock.

or

Mr. William King
regrets that a previous engagement
prevents his acceptance of
Mr. and Mrs. Edward Stanley's
kind invitation
for Tuesday, June nineteenth,
at seven o'clock.

EXERCISE 255

Study carefully the arrangement of items in the foregoing forms, and then copy on note-paper these forms.

EXERCISE 256

(1) Write an invitation to dinner from Mr. and Mrs. Luther Brown to Miss Julia Reed.

(2) Write an answer, accepting the invitation.

(3) Write an answer, declining the invitation.

APPENDIX

—∘o:o:oo—

I

THE ENGLISH LANGUAGE

LANGUAGES that have come from the same original tongue are said to belong to the same family. The English language is a member of the Aryan or Indo-European family of languages. There are two great divisions of the Indo-European family, an Eastern or Asiatic division, and a Western or European division. These include seven branches: Indian (Sanskrit, Hindustani, etc.); Iranian (Persian, etc.); Greek; Italic or Romanic (Latin, and the Romance tongues which have sprung from the Latin, such as Italian, French, Spanish, and Portuguese); Celtic (Welsh, Irish, and Gaelic); Slavonic (Russian, Bulgarian, Polish, Bohemian, etc.); and Teutonic or Germanic (Scandinavian, English, German, etc.).

The principal divisions of the Teutonic or Germanic branch of the Indo-European family are: Scandinavian (Icelandic, Norwegian, Swedish, and Danish); High German, the language originally spoken by the people who dwelt in the highlands of Germany; Low German (Dutch, Flemish, and Anglo-Saxon or English), the language originally spoken by the people who dwelt in the lowlands of

Germany, near the coast. The most important member of the Low-German division of the Teutonic group is English.

The English language, in its earliest form, was introduced into Britain about the middle of the fifth century by the Angles, Saxons, and Jutes, Low-German tribes from the northern part of Germany. These invaders gradually displaced the native population of Britain, and founded kingdoms of their own. They were known to the Britons as Saxons, but they called themselves "English" (*Englisc*), and the land they had won "England" (*Englaland*, the land of the Angles). The language of these Teutonic settlers of Britain became in time the national tongue. This oldest form of our own language is commonly called Anglo-Saxon or Old English.

The ancient Britons belonged to the Celtic race, and spoke the Celtic tongue. As a result of their intercourse with the Angles and Saxons, a few Celtic words came into our language. Among the words of Celtic origin that were adopted from the conquered Britons are the names of articles in common use at that time, such as *basket, cradle, crock, mattock*, and *mop;* and some of the oldest names of rivers, hills, mountains, and towns; as, *Avon, Esk, Dee; Cheviot, Malvern, Ben Nevis; Aberdeen, Liverpool, London.*

The Teutonic settlers in Britain also borrowed from the Britons a few Latin words left by the Romans, who had held Britain from 43 A.D. to 410 A.D. Among these words are *strata* (*via strata*), a paved way, and *castra*, a camp.

They appear in modern English as *street*, *Chester*, *Manchester*, *Lancaster*, *Leicester*.

The introduction of Christianity among the English at the close of the sixth century brought with it the study of Latin, and led to increased communication between England and the other European nations. Hence a great number of Latin words, most of them relating to the church, passed into English; as, *altar*, *bishop*, *creed*, *church*, *clerk*, *deacon*, *priest*, *psalm*, *temple*. Many words of this class had been borrowed by the Romans from Greek, but they came into our language through the Latin tongue. Owing to their extended trade, the English became acquainted at this time with many new things and products, and this brought them such words as *cup*, *fork*, *lobster*, *palm*, *peach*.

Toward the close of the eighth century, Northmen or Danes, from the Scandinavian peninsula and from Denmark, began to make incursions into England. After a time they began to settle there, and, finally, in the eleventh century, held for a time the English throne. Owing to this conquest, and to the consequent close commercial and literary intercourse with Denmark and the Low Dutch coast, some Norse or Scandinavian words were introduced into the English language. Among the number are many names of places ending in *by* (a town); as, *Derby*, *Rugby*, *Whitby*. Proper names ending in *son* are also of Norse origin; as, *Johnson*, *Stephenson*.

While the Danes were making conquests in England, other Northmen settled in northern France, where they were called Normans. Here, in the tenth century, they founded the duchy of Normandy, and gradually adopted the customs and language of the French people. In 1066, the Normans, under William, Duke of Normandy, conquered England.

After the Norman Conquest, French became the language of the English Court and of the higher classes. French was used in Parliament, in the courts of law, and even in the schools. But the great majority of the people continued to speak English. For a time the two languages were spoken, side by side, but gradually the Normans and the English became one people, and spoke one tongue—the English language.

During the long period when the two races were becoming one, a vast body of Norman French words had found their way into English. This element of English is called a Latin element, as the French language, of which the Norman French is a form, is descended from the Latin tongue.

Many different classes of words came into English through the Norman French. The Normans introduced feudalism and the chase into England; they also introduced new methods of warfare and their own system of law. Some of the words that came into the language as a result of this are *homage*, *fealty*, *vassal*, relating to feudalism; *brace*, *chase*, *forest*, *mews*, connected with the chase; *arms*, *battle*, *captain*, *mail*, *vizor*, pertaining to warfare; *attorney*, *court*, *judge*, *justice*, *plaintiff*, *sue*, *trespass*, terms used in the law.

Some of the church terms came to us through the Normans; as, *ceremony*, *miracle*, *penance*, *procession*, *relic*, *tonsure*.

A great number of English titles were introduced by the Normans; as, *count, countess, duke, empress, peer, mayor;* but *king, queen, earl, lord, lady,* and *alderman,* are old English words that were in use before the Norman Conquest.

Certain refinements of life were introduced by the Normans, and hence came such words as *carpet, curtain, mirror, napkin, parlor, table.* Norman French words, like *beef, mutton, pork, veal,* were introduced to designate the flesh of certain animals when used as food; but the old English names, *ox, sheep, swine, calf,* are still used in speaking of the living animals.

Besides the few Latin words that the Teutonic settlers adopted from the Britons, the Latin words that came into English through the introduction of Christianity into Britain, and the great body of Latin words that came into the language indirectly through Norman French, there are many others that found their way into the language at a later period. Owing to the revival of classical study in England, a great number of Latin words came into the language during the sixteenth and seventeenth centuries. Many of these words appeared in the written or printed language, but never passed into general use.

Many Greek words have also come into the language since the beginning of the sixteenth century. Most of our scientific terms are of Greek origin.

The spread of English exploration and the growth of commerce between English-speaking people and people who speak other languages, has brought into English words from the Spanish, Italian, French, German, Dutch, Chinese,

Russian, Persian, Arabic, and many other languages. Many of these words are the names of articles or customs peculiar to the country from which the words were borrowed; as, **Spanish**: *armada, cigar;* **Italian**: *balcony, lava, opera;* **French**: *bouquet, chagrin, programme;* **German**: *kindergarten, meer-schaum, waltz, zinc;* **Dutch**: *skate, sloop, yacht;* **Chinese**: *china, nankeen, tea;* **Russian**: *Czar, drosky, steppe;* **Persian**: *chess, shawl, turban;* **Arabic**: *algebra, coffee, gazelle.*

The English of the present day differs greatly from Anglo-Saxon or Old English. Anglo-Saxon was an inflected language. That is, the relation of words to each other was expressed, as in Latin and Greek, by the endings of the words. Nearly all of these grammatical endings or inflections were gradually lost after the Danish and Norman Conquests, and we now in most cases indicate the relations of words by their position in the sentence, or by distinct words, such as prepositions and auxiliary verbs.

Modern English differs from Old English not only in its lack of inflections, but also in the character of its vocabulary. The language of our Teutonic ancestors was an unmixed speech. It contained no foreign elements. Modern English has in its vocabulary more words of foreign than of native origin. A large majority of these words are from Latin or Greek, many of which are scientific, philosophical, or technical terms. About three-fourths of the words in common use are of Anglo-Saxon origin.

RULES FOR THE USE OF CAPITAL LETTERS AND MARKS OF PUNCTUATION

I. CAPITAL LETTERS

1. The first word of every sentence should begin with a capital letter.

2. A proper name should begin with a capital letter.

3. Nouns or adjectives derived from proper names should usually begin with capital letters.

4. The names of the months and of the days of the week should begin with capital letters.

5. Titles of honor or respect and official titles should begin with capital letters, when they are applied to an individual or are used as part of a name; as, —

The President of the United States, the Governor of New York, the Mayor of Chicago, William the Conqueror, dear Sir.

Queen Victoria, President Lincoln, General Grant.

6. The name of a religious body, or of a political party, should begin with a capital letter; as, —

Roman Catholic, Protestant, Episcopalian, Presbyterian, Methodist, Baptist; Whig, Tory, Democrat, Republican, Conservative, Liberal.

7. The important words in the title of a book, of a newspaper, or of any other composition should begin with capital letters; as, —

The Jungle Book, New York Evening Post, In the White Mountains.

8. All names and titles of the Deity should begin with capital letters; as, —

Lord, God, Creator, Father, the Supreme Being.

9. The pronoun *I* and the interjection *O* should be written or printed in capital letters; as, —

O father! I see a gleaming light.

10. The first word of a direct quotation should begin with a capital letter; as, —

He replied, " Kindness wins friends."

11. The first word of every line of poetry should begin with a capital letter.

II. MARKS OF PUNCTUATION

THE PERIOD

1. A complete sentence, not interrogative or exclamatory, should be followed by a period.

2. Every abbreviated word should be followed by a period; as, —

Mr., Mrs., Dr., Hon., Rev.

The Interrogation Point

An interrogative sentence should be followed by the interrogation point; as, —

> What will be the result?

The Exclamation Point

An exclamatory word, phrase, or sentence should be followed by the exclamation point; as, —

Hark! I hear footsteps. O noble judge! What a wonderful gift he possesses!

The Comma

1. The name of a person or thing addressed should be separated from the rest of the sentence by a comma or commas; as, —

Come with me, John. Ring, happy bells, across the snow.

2. A series of words, phrases, or clauses in the same construction should be separated by commas; as, —

He was an honest, temperate, forgiving man. I come to bury Cæsar, not to praise him. She knew how far she could go, and what she could do.

NOTE. — Two words in the same construction, or two short phrases connected by *and*, *or*, or *nor*, should not be separated by the comma; as, *He was brave and patriotic.*

3. A transposed phrase or clause is usually separated from the rest of the sentence by a comma; as, —

In a very short time, they had passed the spot. If we fail, you will be disappointed.

NOTE. — If the phrase is closely united with the sentence, the comma is not used; as, *Beneath the window is a wooden bench.*

4. An appositive word or phrase is usually separated from the rest of the sentence by a comma or commas; as, —

> Milton, the great English poet, was blind.

But when the explanatory term combines closely with the word explained, the comma is omitted; as, —

The outlet of this lake is the river Nile. The emperor Augustus was a patron of the fine arts.

5. Words, phrases, or clauses placed between closely related parts of a sentence should be separated from the rest of the sentence by commas; as, —

> It is mind, after all, which does the work of the world.

6. A relative clause not restrictive should be separated from the remainder of the sentence by the comma; as, —

Cherish true patriotism, which has its root in benevolence.

7. The comma is often used to indicate an omission of a word or words; as, —

> Labor brings pleasure; idleness, pain.

8. A short quotation, informally introduced, should be separated from the preceding part of the sentence by a comma; as, —

Agassiz once said, "I have no time to waste in making money."

9. The members of a compound sentence, when short and closely connected, should be separated by the comma; as, —

> He whistled shrill, and he was answered from the hill.

The Semicolon

1. When the members of a compound sentence are subdivided by the comma, they are usually separated by the semicolon; as, —

If I ever saw the creature, it was a long, long while ago; and, to tell you the truth, I doubt whether I ever did see him.

2. Short clauses, slightly connected in meaning and not joined by conjunctions, should be separated by the semicolon; as, —

The old men sit at their doors; the gossip leans over her counter; the children shout and frolic in the streets.

The Colon

When a speech or quotation is formally introduced by *thus*, *as follows*, *these words*, or some similar expression, it should be preceded by a colon; as, —

Carlyle used these words: "Be true, if you would be believed."

Marks of Parenthesis

Marks of parenthesis are used to enclose words or expressions which do not strictly belong to the sentence; as, —

Nor did I fail (as is the custom of landed proprietors all about the world) to parade the poor fellow up and down over my half a dozen acres.

The Dash

1. The dash is often used instead of marks of parenthesis to enclose parenthetical expressions that are closely related to the whole sentence; as, —

A room with seven doors — like the famous apartment in Washington's headquarters at Newburgh — is an invitation to bewilderment.

2. The dash is used to mark an abrupt change in thought or in the construction of a sentence; as, —

She happened to cast her eyes over a great, broad field of waving grain — and whom do you think she saw?

Hast thou — but how shall I ask a question which must bring tears into so many eyes?

Quotation Marks

Every direct quotation should be enclosed by quotation marks. When the quotation is divided by other words, each part should be enclosed by quotation marks; as, —

" Have you anything to tell me, little bird? " asked Ulysses.

" Peep ! " said the bird, " peep, peep, pe-weep ! "

The Hyphen

1. The hyphen is used to join the parts of a compound word; as, —

man-of-war   twenty-three   crab-apple

2. To join the syllables of a word divided at the end of a line.

III

LIST OF ABBREVIATIONS

@ . . . . At or to.
A.B. or B.A . . . Bachelor of Arts.
acct. . . . . Account.
A.D. . . . In the year of our Lord.
Ala. . . . . Alabama.
A.M. (*Ante Meridiem*) Before noon.
A.M. . . In the year of the world.
A.M. or M.A. . . Master of Arts.
Anon. . . . . . . Anonymous.
Ark. . . . . Arkansas.
Ariz. . . . . . . Arizona Territory.
Aug. . . . . August.
Av. or Ave . . . . Avenue.
B.C. . . . . . . Before Christ.
Bp. . . . . Bishop.
Cal. . . . . California.
Capt. . . . . Captain.
Co. . . . . Company.
Co. . . . . County.
C.O.D. . . . Collect on Delivery.
Col. . . . . Colonel.
Coll. . . . . College.
Colo. or Col. . . . . Colorado.
Conn. . . . . Connecticut.
Cor. Sec., Corresponding Secretary.
Cr. . . . . Credit.
Cr. . . . . Creditor.
ct. . . . . cent.
D.C. . . . . District of Columbia.

D.D. . . . . Doctor of Divinity.
Dec. . . . . December.
Del. . . . . Delaware.
Del. (*Delineavit*) He or she drew it.
do. (*ditto*) . . . . The same.
Dr. . . . . Debtor.
Dr. . . . . Doctor.
E. . . . . East.
e.g. (*exempli gratia*) . For example.
Esq. . . . . Esquire.
etc. or &c., And others; and so forth.
Ex. . . . . Example.
F. or Fahr.,
                Fahrenheit (thermometer).
Feb. . . . . February.
Fla. . . . . Florida.
Fri. . . . . Friday.
F.R.S., Fellow of the Royal Society.
Ga. . . . . Georgia.
Gen. . . . . General.
Gov. . . . . . . Governor.
Gov.-Gen. . . Governor-General.
Hon. . . . . . . Honorable.
Idaho . . . . Idaho.
i.e. (*id est*) . . . . . That is.
Ill. . . . . Illinois.
Ind. . . . . Indiana.
Ind. T. . . . . Indian Territory.
inst., Instant — the present month.

Iowa or Io.	. . . . . .	Iowa.
Jan.	. . . .	January.
Jr. or Jun.	. . . . . .	Junior.
Kans. or Kan.	. . . .	Kansas.
Ky.	. . . .	Kentucky.
La.	. . . .	Louisiana.
L.I.	. . . . . .	Long Island.
Lieut.	. . . . . .	Lieutenant.
Lieut.-Col.	.	Lieutenant-Colonel.
Lieut.-Gen.	.	Lieutenant-General.
Lieut.-Gov.		Lieutenant-Governor.
LL.D.	. . .	Doctor of Laws.
M. (*meridies*)	. . . . .	Noon.
Maj.-Gen.	. . .	Major-General.
Mass.	. . . . . .	Massachusetts.
M.C.	. . .	Member of Congress.
M.D.	. . .	Doctor of Medicine.
Md.	. . . .	Maryland.
Me.	. . . .	Maine.
Messrs. (*Messieurs*)	.	Gentlemen.
Mich.	. . . . . .	Michigan.
Minn.	. . . . . .	Minnesota.
Miss.	. . . . . .	Mississippi.
Mlle.	. . . . . .	Mademoiselle.
Mme.	. . . . . .	Madame.
Mo.	. . . .	Missouri.
Mon.	. . . .	Monday.
Mont.	. . . . . .	Montana.
M.P.	. . .	Member of Parliament.
Mr.	. . . .	Mister.
Mrs.	. . . .	Mistress.
Ms.	. . . .	Manuscript.
Mss.	. . . . . .	Manuscripts.
Mt.	. . . .	Mount.
N.	. . . .	North.
N.A.	. . . .	North America.
N.B. (*nota bene*)	. . .	Note well.
Nebr. or Neb.	. . .	Nebraska.
Nev.	. . . .	Nevada.

N.C.	. . . .	North Carolina.
N. Dak.	. . . . .	North Dakota.
N.H.	. . . . .	New Hampshire.
N.J.	. . . . . .	New Jersey.
N. Mex.	. . . .	New Mexico.
No.	. . . .	Number.
Nov.	. . . . . .	November.
N.Y.	. . . . .	New York.
Oct.	. . . . . .	October.
Ohio or O.	. . . . . .	Ohio.
Okla. T.	. . .	Oklahoma Territory.
Or.	. . . .	Oregon.
p.	. . . .	Page.
Pa. or Penn.	. . .	Pennsylvania.
per cent (*per centum*)		
		By the hundred.
Ph.D.	. . .	Doctor of Philosophy.
Pinx. (*Pinxit*)	.	He or she painted it.
P.M. (*post meridiem*)	.	Afternoon.
P.M.	. . . .	Postmaster.
P.O.	. . . . . .	Post-office.
pp.	. . . .	Pages.
Pres.	. . . . . .	President.
Prof.	. . . . . .	Professor.
Pro tem. (*pro tempore*)		
		For the time being.
prox. (*proximo*)	. .	Next month.
P.S. (*post scriptum*)	.	Postscript.
Rev.	. . . . . .	Reverend.
R.I.	. . . . .	Rhode Island.
R.R.	. . . . . .	Railroad.
Rt. Rev.	. . .	Right Reverend.
S.	. . . .	South.
Sat.	. . . . . .	Saturday.
Sept.	. . . . . .	September.
Sr. or Sen.	. . . . .	Senior.
S.C.	. . . .	South Carolina.
S. Dak.	. . . .	South Dakota.
St.	. . . .	Street.

Sun.	Sunday.
Supt.	Superintendent.
Tenn.	Tennessee.
Tex.	Texas.
Thurs.	Thursday.
Tues.	Tuesday.
ult. (*ultimo*)	Last month.
U.S.	United States.
U.S.A.	United States Army.
U.S.A.	United States of America.
U.S.M.	United States Mail.
U.S.N.	United States Navy.
Utah	Utah.
Va.	Virginia.
viz. (*videlicet*)	To wit, namely.
vs. (*versus*)	Against.
Vt.	Vermont.
W.	West.
Wash.	Washington.
Wed.	Wednesday.
Wis.	Wisconsin.
W. Va.	West Virginia.
Wyo.	Wyoming.

IV

PARTS OF A SENTENCE

Some grammarians divide a sentence into three parts —
the *subject*, the *predicate*, and the *copula*.[1] Thus, in the
sentence, " Ice is cold," they call *ice* the subject, *cold* the
predicate, and *is* the copula. The subject names the thing,
ice, about which something is said; the predicate expresses
what is affirmed of the subject; and the copula joins the
subject with the predicate and expresses the assertion.

Many verbs, such as *be, become, seem*, cannot form logical
predicates by themselves, but require the help of another
word, usually a noun or an adjective, to express the idea
asserted. The verb *be*, in most of its uses,[2] has no meaning of its own, but serves to connect its subject to a word
or words describing the subject. Thus, in the sentences,
" He is a soldier" and " He is brave," the verb *is* merely
joins the subject with the predicate and expresses the
assertion.

Other verbs, which both assert and express the idea
asserted, may be resolved into the copula and a predicate;
thus, " He *runs* " into " He *is running*."

---

[1] See pages 106 and 136.   [2] See page 136.

INDEX

323